Cochrane
Marigold Library System
NOV - - 2012

D0580170

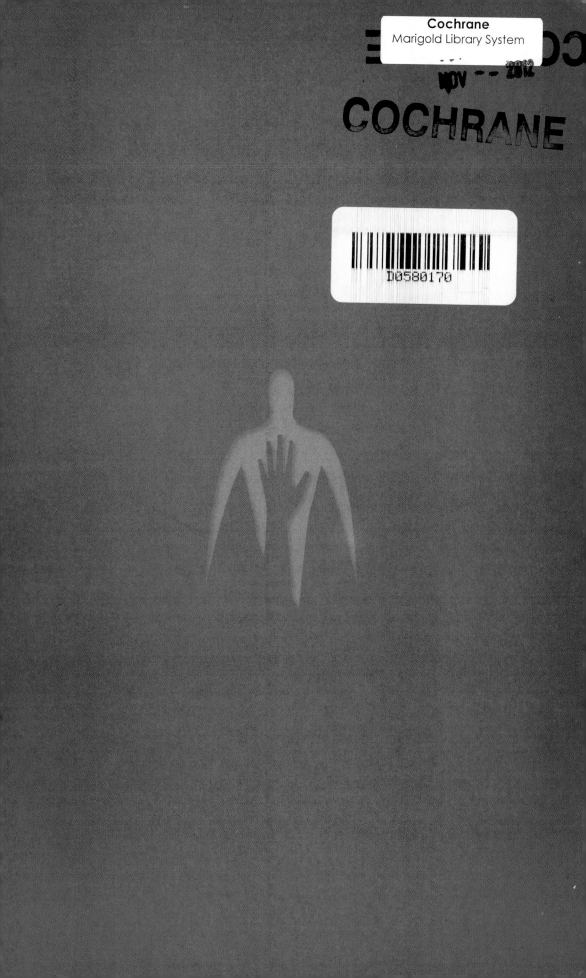

THE

SURRO

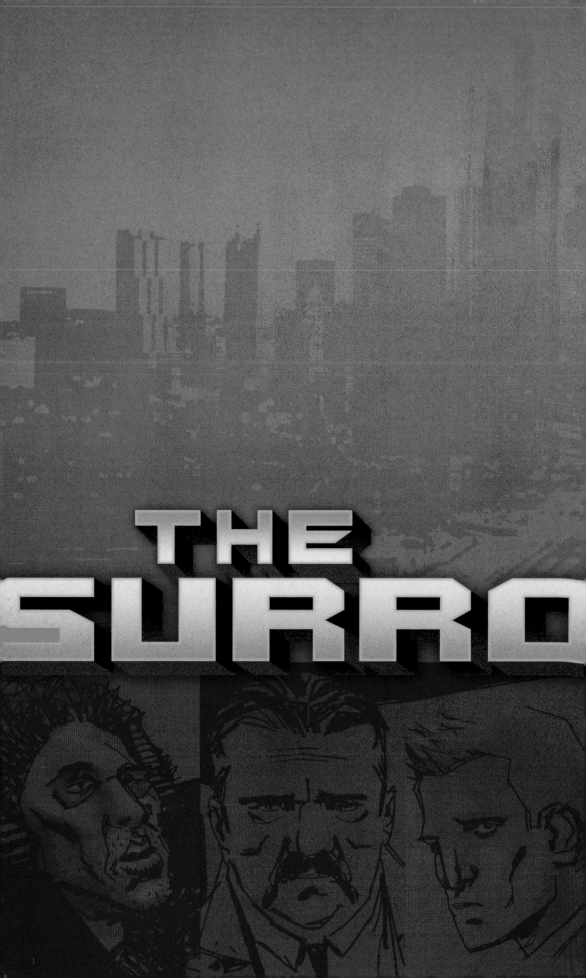

CREATED AND WRITTEN BY
ROBERT VENDITTI

ILLUSTRATED AND COLORED BY
BRETT WELDELE

EDITED BY
CHRIS STAROS

BOOK DESIGN BY
BISSEL & TITUS
WWW.BISSELTITUS.COM

Published by Top Shelf Productions,
PO Box 1282, Marietta, GA 30061-1282, USA.
Publishers: Chris Staros and Brett Warnock.

Third Printing, July 2009.
Printed in China.

Visit our online catalog at
www.topshelfcomix.com

ISBN 978-1-891830-87-7
1. Graphic Novels
2. Science Fiction

Top Shelf Productions

chapter
ONE

Field Test

hogan's tavern

WHAT ARE YOU DOING?
I WANT TO CHECK OUT WHAT'S DOWN THIS ALLEY.

SURE. I KNOW WHAT *YOU* WANT TO CHECK OUT, BUT I DON'T THINK THIS IS THE BEST WEATHER FOR IT.

BE ADVENTUROUS. IT'S NOT LIKE YOU'RE GOING TO CATCH A COLD OR ANYTHING.

BUT WHAT IF SOMEBODY SEES US?

WHO *CARES*? WE WORK HARD FOR THESE BODIES. MIGHT AS WELL SHOW THEM OFF.

BESIDES, WE'LL BE IN AND OUT BEFORE ANYONE NOTICES. I PROMISE.
YOU SURE KNOW WHAT A GIRL LIKES TO HEAR, *ROMEO* . . .
BUT I THINK I'D RATHER GO SOMEPLACE MORE PRIVATE.

ON THE OTHER HAND, I *SUPPOSE* I COULD LOOSEN UP JUST THIS--

SOMEONE'S COMING.
NOT YET, BUT GIMME A SEC--

NO. SOMEONE'S *COMING*.

YOU MIND?
THE LADY WOULD LIKE SOME PRIVACY.

CENTRAL GEORGIA METROPOLIS.

BACKBONE DISTRICT.

MAY 8, 2054.

hagan's tavern
CGM
POLICE

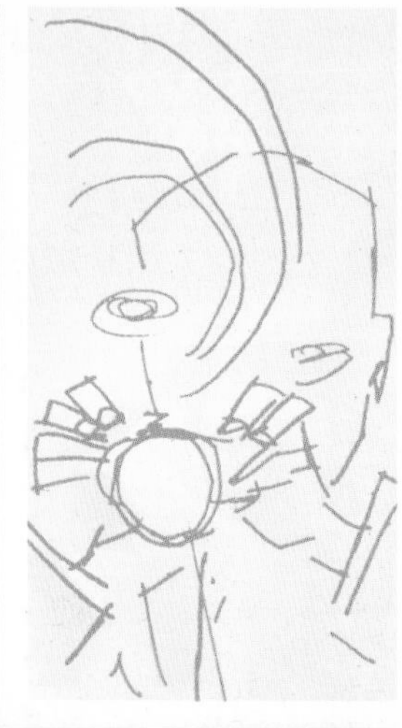

SORRY, SERGEANT.
TAKE FIVE, WILL YOU, ART? THESE TWO AREN'T GOING ANYWHERE.

BEEP

RETRIEVING REGISTRY

JACKOWSKI, HENRY A

WHAT'VE WE GOT, PETE?

HEY, HARV.
LOOKS LIKE A COUPLE OF FRYJOBS. A FLASH STORM MOVED THROUGH ABOUT A HALF-HOUR AGO. GUY WALKING BY SAYS HE SAW SPARKS SHOOTING OUT OF THE ALLEY LIKE IT WAS THE FOURTH OF JULY.

I DON'T SUPPOSE THESE TWO WERE JUST PASSING BY.
YEAH, RIGHT.
THE MALE HAD A RECEIPT FROM HOGAN'S BAR, TIME-STAMPED JUST BEFORE THE STORM. GUESS THEY DUCKED IN HERE FOR A LITTLE POSTGAME WRAP-UP.

NOTHING LOOSENS AN OPERATOR'S INHIBITIONS LIKE A LITTLE SIMULATED INTOXICATION. WHO DO THEY BELONG TO?
SURROGATE NUMBER ONE'S REGISTERED TO A HENRY A. JACKOWSKI, BLOCK 2413, BUILDING 9, UNIT 836.

WHAT ABOUT THE FEMALE?
THAT **WAS** THE FEMALE.

I'VE GOT TO GET OUT OF THIS PRECINCT.
THOUGHT YOU'D LIKE THAT. NUMBER TWO BELONGS TO AN EDWARD T. CLEGG. LIVES RIGHT HERE IN THE BACKBONE.

YOU GOT EVERYTHING YOU NEED FOR THE REPORT?
IT'S PRETTY OPEN-AND-SHUT. ART'S GOING TO FINISH TAKING PICTURES FOR THE INSURANCE GUYS.

ALRIGHT. SEND A COUPLE OF UNIFORMS AROUND TO MR. JACKOWSKI'S. I'M IN NO MOOD FOR THAT.
WE'LL NOTIFY CLEGG AND SEE WHAT HE'S GOT TO SAY.
THEY'RE ALL YOURS, ART.

GO AWAY!

MR. CLEGG? IT'S LIEUTENANT GREER AND SERGEANT FORD WITH METRO POLICE. WE NEED A MINUTE OF YOUR TIME.

SORRY TO DISTURB YOU, MR. CLEGG, BUT ARE YOU THE OWNER/OPERATOR OF A SURROGATE SERIAL NUMBERED D4C-7NPZ?
YEAH.
COME ON IN.

WE'RE HERE TO INFORM YOU THAT YOUR SURROGATE WAS DISABLED DURING A FLASH STORM IN THE BACKBONE DISTRICT THIS EVENING.
I KNOW. I WAS THERE. HOW BAD IS THE DAMAGE?

WE'RE WAITING FOR THE FORENSIC EXAMINER'S REPORT, BUT IT LOOKS LIKE A TOTAL LOSS.

OH, GOD! I JUST PURCHASED IT. TOP-OF-THE-LINE MODEL WITH DATA RECORDING AND PLAYBACK. I HAVEN'T EVEN MADE THE FIRST PAYMENT YET!
WE'RE SORRY, MR. CLEGG. WE'LL TRY TO SPEED ALONG THE INSURANCE PROCESS AS MUCH AS POSS--

WHAT INSURANCE? I WAS WAITING TO BUY A POLICY WITH MY NEXT PAYCHECK. NOW WHAT AM I GOING TO DO?
I'VE GOT A JOB AS A CONSTRUCTION WORKER, FOR CHRIST'S SAKE! DOES IT LOOK LIKE I'M READY FOR MANUAL LABOR?

DO YOU HAVE A PRIOR SURROGATE YOU CAN USE?
I TRADED IT IN AS A DOWN PAYMENT ON THE NEW ONE.
WHAT HAPPENED TO TRUDY?

TRUDY WOULD BE THE FEMALE SURROGATE REGISTERED TO HENRY JACKOWSKI? THAT UNIT APPEARS TO BE A TOTAL LOSS AS WELL.
WHO THE *HELL* IS HENRY JACKOWSKI? YOU MEAN TRUDY WAS A *MAN*?

YOU DIDN'T KNOW?
OF *COURSE* I DIDN'T KNOW! WHAT DO YOU TAKE ME FOR?

WHY CAN'T PEOPLE JUST BE WHO THEY SAY THEY ARE?
I WAS WONDERING THE SAME THING.
THIS KEEPS GETTING BETTER. AT LEAST TELL ME THAT OTHER GUY GOT FRIED, TOO.

WHAT OTHER--
I THINK WE'VE TAKEN ENOUGH OF YOUR TIME, MR. CLEGG. WE'LL JUST NEED A COPY OF THE DISK FOR OUR RECORDS, AND THEN WE'LL BE ON OUR WAY.

DISK?

THE *DISK*. OR AM I TO BELIEVE YOU BROKE THE BANK ON A TOP-OF-THE-LINE SURROGATE--COMPLETE WITH DATA RECORDING AND PLAYBACK--BUT DIDN'T DOCUMENT ITS FIRST DATE FOR FUTURE . . . ENJOYMENT?

OKAY, OKAY. YOU CAN HAVE THE ORIGINAL, FOR ALL I CARE. THE EVENING ENDED BEFORE WE GOT TO THE GOOD STUFF, ANYWAY.

WE APPRECIATE YOUR COOPERATION, MR. CLEGG. SOMEONE FROM FORENSICS WILL CONTACT YOU WHEN THEIR EXAMINATION IS COMPLETE.
AW, WHAT'S THE USE . . .

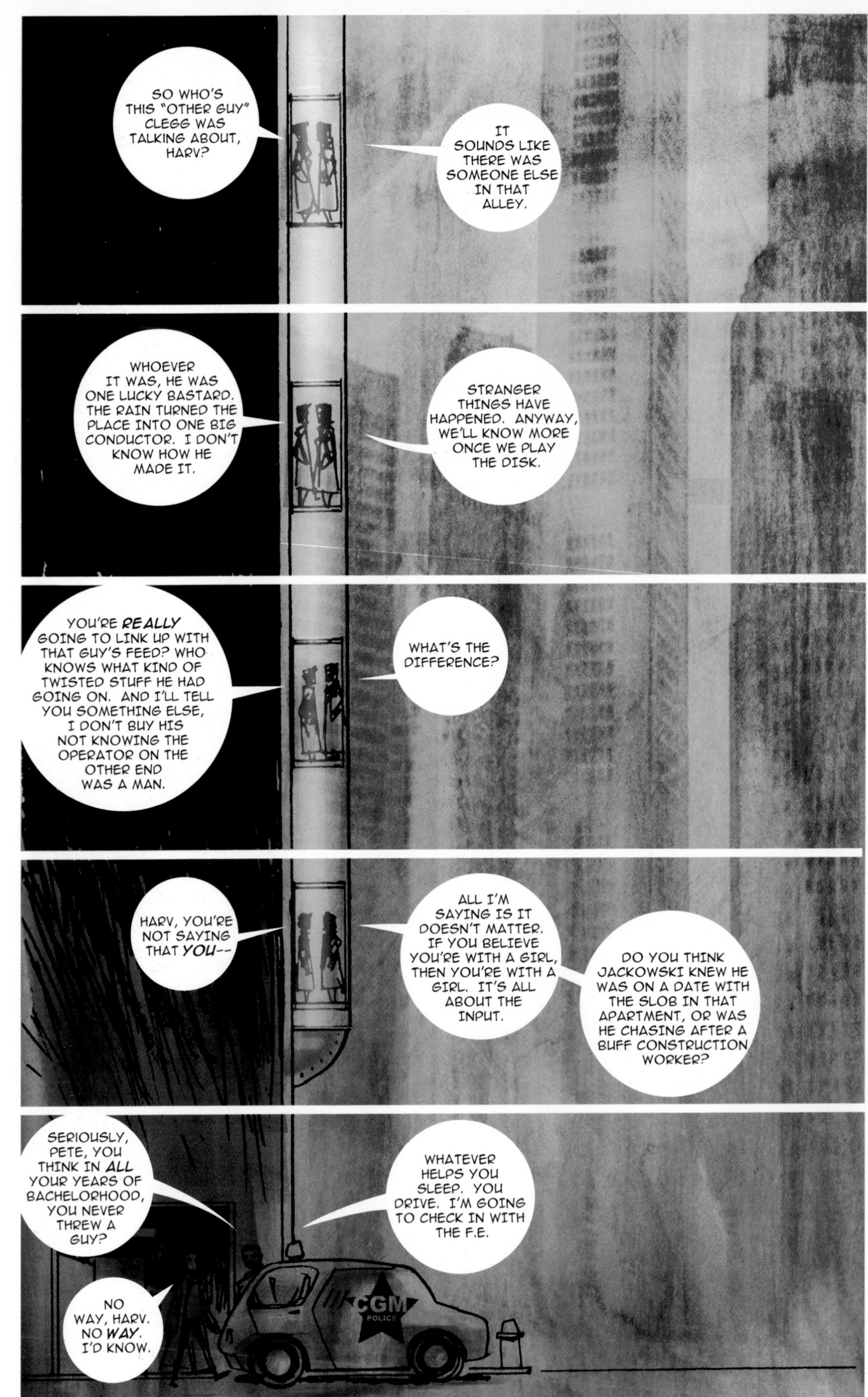
SO WHO'S THIS "OTHER GUY" CLEGG WAS TALKING ABOUT, HARV?
IT SOUNDS LIKE THERE WAS SOMEONE ELSE IN THAT ALLEY.
WHOEVER IT WAS, HE WAS ONE LUCKY BASTARD. THE RAIN TURNED THE PLACE INTO ONE BIG CONDUCTOR. I DON'T KNOW HOW HE MADE IT.
STRANGER THINGS HAVE HAPPENED. ANYWAY, WE'LL KNOW MORE ONCE WE PLAY THE DISK.
YOU'RE ***REALLY*** GOING TO LINK UP WITH THAT GUY'S FEED? WHO KNOWS WHAT KIND OF TWISTED STUFF HE HAD GOING ON. AND I'LL TELL YOU SOMETHING ELSE, I DON'T BUY HIS NOT KNOWING THE OPERATOR ON THE OTHER END WAS A MAN.
WHAT'S THE DIFFERENCE?
HARV, YOU'RE NOT SAYING THAT ***YOU***--
ALL I'M SAYING IS IT DOESN'T MATTER. IF YOU BELIEVE YOU'RE WITH A GIRL, THEN YOU'RE WITH A GIRL. IT'S ALL ABOUT THE INPUT.
DO YOU THINK JACKOWSKI KNEW HE WAS ON A DATE WITH THE SLOB IN THAT APARTMENT, OR WAS HE CHASING AFTER A BUFF CONSTRUCTION WORKER?
SERIOUSLY, PETE, YOU THINK IN ***ALL*** YOUR YEARS OF BACHELORHOOD, YOU NEVER THREW A GUY?
WHATEVER HELPS YOU SLEEP. YOU DRIVE. I'M GOING TO CHECK IN WITH THE F.E.
CGM
POLICE
NO WAY, HARV. NO ***WAY***. I'D KNOW.

BACKBONE PRECINCT. FORENSIC EXAMINER.

EVENING, LIEUTENANT GREER.
HEY, SCREWS. DID THE SCRAP WAGON DROP OFF TWO SURRIES FOR ME?

YEAH, I GOT 'EM. BOTH FRY-JOBS. NO DOUBT ABOUT IT.
NO SURPRISE THERE. ANY SALVAGE VALUE?

NONE. I'VE NEVER SEEN ANYTHING LIKE IT. CHIPS AND CIRCUITRY ARE SHOT TO HELL. SOME OF THE WIRING IS ACTUALLY *WELDED* TO THE CHASSIS. HAD TO BE A DIRECT HIT.
I'M SENDING YOU SOME IMAGES.

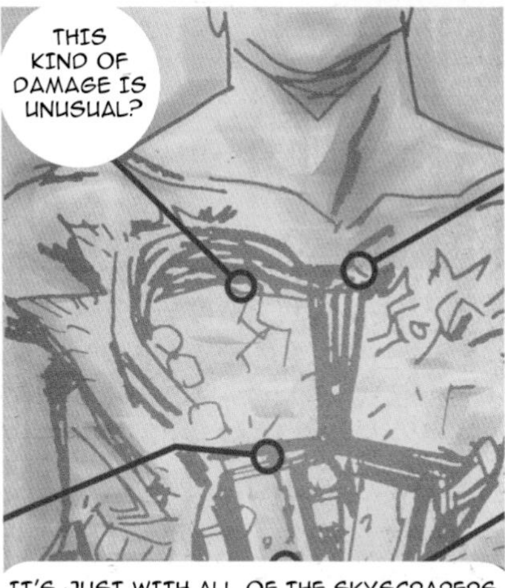
THIS KIND OF DAMAGE IS UNUSUAL?
IT'S JUST WITH ALL OF THE SKYSCRAPERS AND RADIO ANTENNAS IN THE BACKBONE, THE CHANCE OF A LIGHTNING BOLT MAKING IT ALL THE WAY TO THE GROUND IS LIKE GETTING BIT BY A SHARK WHILE HOLDING THE WINNING LOTTO TICKET. I'VE HEARD OF IT HAPPENING BEFORE, BUT . . .

WHAT WERE THEY DOING IN THAT ALLEY ANYWAY?
DO I HAVE TO DRAW YOU A PICTURE?

THAT'S NOT WHAT I MEAN. BURN PATTERNS ON THE COSMETICS SUGGEST THE HANDS WERE THE ELECTRICITY'S POINT OF ENTRY. WERE THEY SWINGING FROM A FLAGPOLE OR SOMETHING?
WHAT CAN I TELL YOU, SCREWS? TO EACH HIS OWN. ANYTHING ELSE?

THAT'S IT. I WAS JUST ABOUT TO CLOSE SHOP.
OKAY. CALL THE OWNER/ OPERATORS AND INFORM THEM THEY CAN PICK UP THEIR SURRIES, THOUGH, UNLESS THEY NEED EXTRA DOORSTOPS, I DON'T KNOW WHY THEY'D BOTHER. AND SCREWS?

YEAH?
DON'T ASK THEM ABOUT THE HANDS.
YOU GOT IT, LIEUTENANT. I'LL SEND YOU THE REPORT WHEN I'M DONE.

WHAT'S THE DEAL WITH THE HANDS?
I DON'T KNOW, BUT I'M STARTING TO WONDER IF THIS ISN'T AS OPEN-AND-SHUT AS WE THOUGHT.

CLEGG DIDN'T STRIKE ME AS THE SORT TO MAKE ENEMIES, SO LET'S RULE HIM OUT AS A CATALYST FOR NOW.
WHY DON'T YOU FIND OUT WHAT YOU CAN ABOUT JACKOWSKI. TALK TO THE UNIFORMS WE SENT BY. DIG INTO THE DATABASE IF YOU HAVE TO. TRY AND FIND A REASON FOR SOMEONE TO ORCHESTRATE WHAT HAPPENED TONIGHT.
I'LL PLAY THE DISK AND SEE IF THIS MYSTERY GUY WAS SOMEHOW INVOLVED.
CGM
POLICE

HOW COME I ALWAYS GET STUCK WITH THE FREAKS, HARV?
BECAUSE YOU'VE GOT SUCH A KNACK FOR IT.

I'M FLATTERED. WELL, AT LEAST IT LOOKS LIKE THINGS ARE GOING TO BE A LITTLE LESS BORING.
I LIKE BOREDOM, PETE. THE MORE BORING OUR JOB IS, THE LESS BAD THINGS ARE HAPPENING IN THE WORLD.

C G M
POLICE
DEPARTMENT
SAY WHAT YOU WANT, OLD-TIMER, BUT I WON'T MIND HAVING A REAL CASE FOR A CHANGE.
BE CAREFUL WHAT YOU WISH FOR, SERGEANT. YOU JUST MIGHT GET IT.

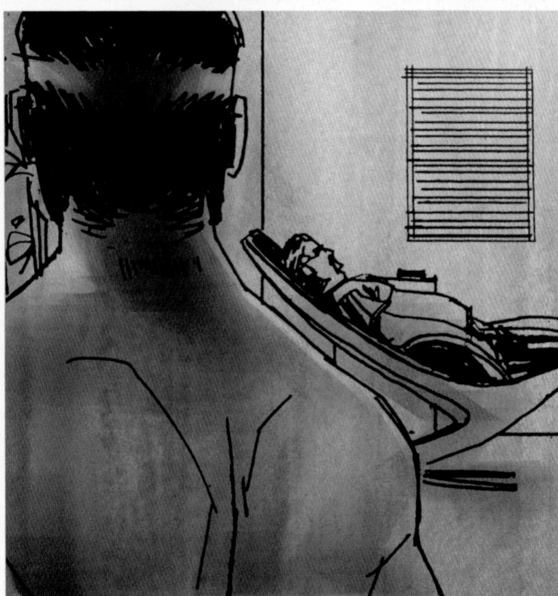
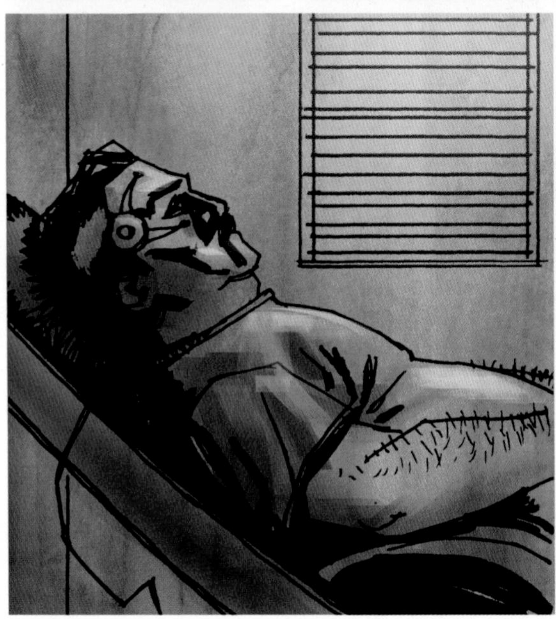

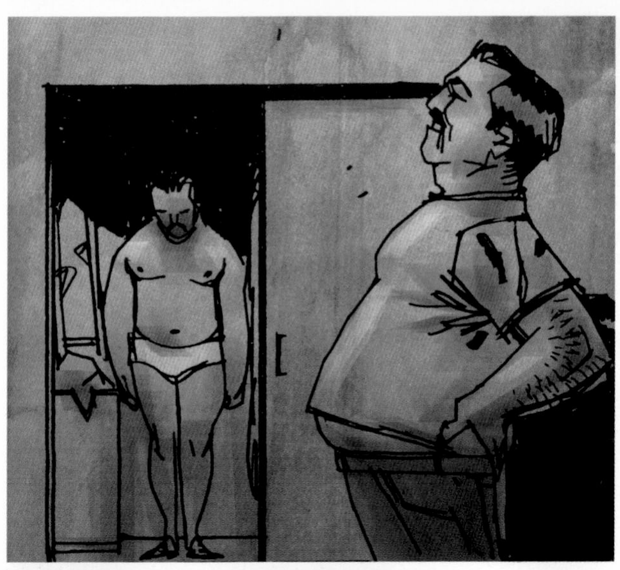

MARGARET?
JUST A MINUTE!

HI, HONEY. DID YOU HAVE A LONG--

OH! WHERE'S YOUR SURROGATE?
I PUT IT UP ALREADY. I KNOW IT'S LATE, BUT I THOUGHT MAYBE WE COULD HAVE DINNER TOGETHER.

I SUPPOSE I COULD STAND TO BE A LITTLE TIRED TOMORROW. GO LINK BACK UP, AND I'LL MEET YOU AT THE TABLE.
NO, MARGARET. I MEAN *TOGETHER* TOGETHER.

DON'T BE RIDICULOUS, HARVEY.
BY THE TIME I GOT MYSELF READY, IT'D BE *BREAKFAST*! DON'T WORRY, I'LL WARM ENOUGH FOOD TO BRING BACK TO THE ROOMS.

IT'S NOT THAT. WE JUST HAVEN'T SAT TOGETHER IN AWHILE. FOR THAT MATTER, IT'S BEEN AWHILE SINCE WE, THE *REAL* WE--
I *DON'T* LIKE THAT KIND OF TALK. NOW DO YOU WANT TO HAVE DINNER WITH ME OR NOT?

NEVERMIND. I'VE GOT SOME WORK TO FINISH UP.
FINE! THERE'LL BE LEFTOVERS IN THE FRIDGE IF YOU WANT THEM!

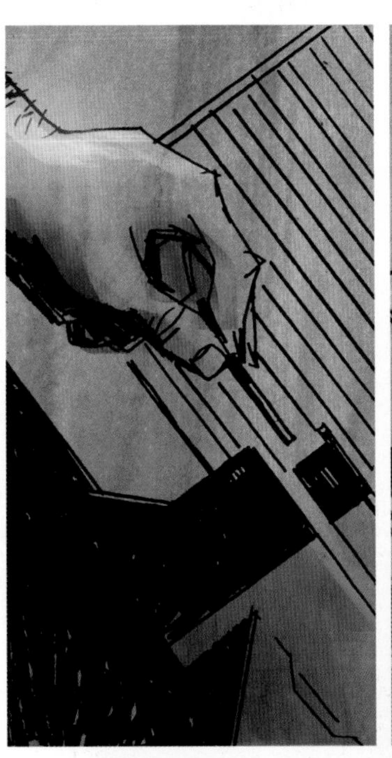

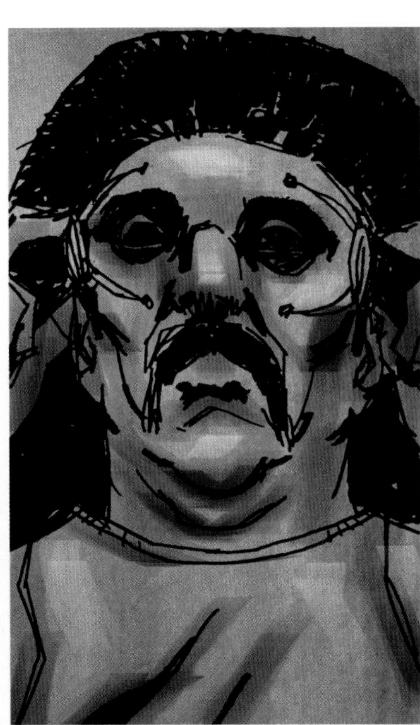

I KNOW WHAT *YOU* WANT TO CHECK OUT--

YOU SURE KNOW WHAT A GIRL LIKES TO HEAR, *ROMEO* . . .

I *SUPPOSE* I COULD LOOSEN UP JUST THIS--

SOMEONE'S COMING.

LIVE.

AFTERNOON, PETE. WHAT'D YOU FIND OUT?
C G M POLICE DEPARTMENT

PETE?

SORRY, HARV. I WAS ON THE CAN.
WELCOME BACK. WHAT'D YOU FIND OUT?

NOTHING . . . UH . . . IMPORTANT.

THE UNIFORMS HAD AN INTERESTING STORY. THEY DROP BY JACKOWSKI'S TO TELL HIM WHAT'S HAPPENED, AND WHO COMES TO THE DOOR BUT A 6'6" MOUNTAIN, LOOKING LIKE HE CAN BENCH PRESS A BUILDING, AND HE'S BAWLING BECAUSE HE CAN'T BE A WOMAN ANYMORE.

WONDERFUL.
ISN'T IT? THEY THOUGHT HE SOUNDED GENUINELY HEARTBROKEN, BUT I CHECKED JUST TO BE SURE.

HE'S CURRENT ON HIS PAYMENTS, AND IT'S A RELATIVELY NEW UNIT, SO THE INSURANCE PAYOUT IS BARELY ENOUGH TO COVER THE BALANCE. NOT MUCH MOTIVE THERE.

OTHER THAN A CITATION FOR PUBLIC LEWDNESS-- GO FIGURE-- HE HAS NO RECORD. HE SELLS WOMEN'S CLOTHES AT AN UPSCALE BOUTIQUE IN THE FASHION DISTRICT. HIS BOSS SAID, AND I QUOTE, "FOR A MAN, TRUDY SURE KNOWS HOW TO MOVE DRESSES."
A TOUCHING EPITAPH.

THAT BRINGS US TO THE F.E.'S REPORT. ASIDE FROM WHAT SCREWS TOLD US LAST NIGHT, NOTHING UNUSUAL. THE ABDOMINAL RESERVOIRS ON BOTH UNITS WERE SWIMMING IN BOOZE, BUT WE EXPECTED AS MUCH.

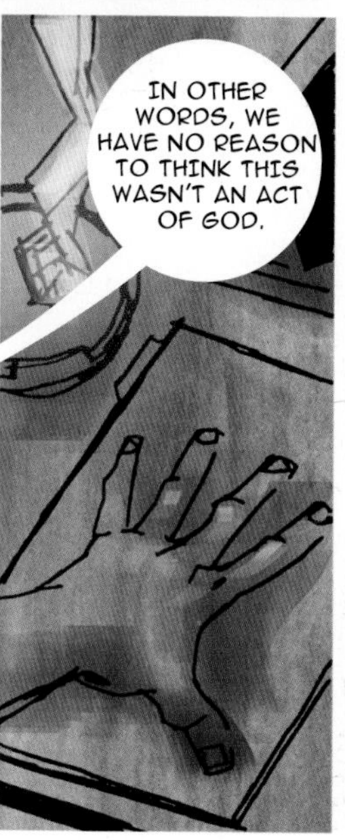
IN OTHER WORDS, WE HAVE NO REASON TO THINK THIS WASN'T AN ACT OF GOD.

WE DO NOW.
COME ON. AND LEAVE THE CIGARETTE.

BUT I JUST LIT IT!
RELAX. IT DOESN'T MAKE YOU LOOK AS SUAVE AS YOU THINK.

I COPIED THIS IMAGE FROM CLEGG'S DISK.

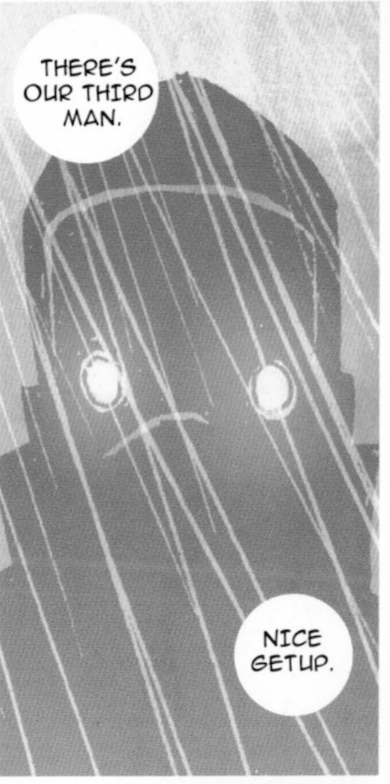
THERE'S OUR THIRD MAN.
NICE GETUP.

HE APPROACHED CLEGG AND JACKOWSKI FROM INSIDE THE ALLEY AND INITIATED AN ALTERCATION. CLEGG TRIED TO RESPOND, FOR ALL THE GOOD IT DID HIM.
YOU REMEMBER WHAT SCREWS SAID ABOUT THE BURN PATTERNS ON THE HANDS? WELL OUR GUY TOOK EACH OF THE SURRIES BY THE HAND JUST BEFORE THEY WERE DISABLED.

HE WAS HOLDING THEIR HANDS?
YEAH. HE'S GOT QUITE A GRIP, TOO. FELT LIKE HE WAS GOING TO SNAP MY FINGERS.

THE WAY I FIGURE IT, ONE OF TWO THINGS HAPPENED NEXT. EITHER HE SUFFERED THE LIGHTNING BOLT'S DIRECT HIT AND MANAGED TO WALK AWAY, DESPITE CLEGG AND JACKOWSKI BOTH GETTING FRIED--

--OR HE SOMEHOW PRODUCED AND DELIVERED THE CHARGE HIMSELF. I'M LEANING TOWARDS THE LATTER, BASED ON SOMETHING HE SAID.

WHICH WAS?
HE TOLD THEM TO "LIVE."

"LIVE?" WHAT THE HELL DOES *THAT* MEAN?
I DON'T KNOW, BUT THERE MUST BE SOMETHING WE'RE NOT SEEING. WHY CLEGG AND JACKOWSKI? WHAT'S THE CONNECTION?

WHAT IF THERE ISN'T A CONNECTION? THIS *COULD* BE A RANDOM ATTACK.
THERE HASN'T BEEN AN UNPROVOKED ATTACK AGAINST A SURROGATE SINCE THE RIOTS OF '39. WHAT END WOULD IT SERVE NOW?
Georgia Dome
Woodruff Park

FIELD TEST.
HM?

A FIELD TEST.
IF WHAT YOU'RE SAYING IS TRUE, THEN OUR ASSAILANT WOULD HAVE TO BE CAPABLE OF DISCHARGING LARGE AMOUNTS OF ELECTRICITY, WHILE AT THE SAME TIME INSULATING HIMSELF FROM ITS EFFECTS, RIGHT?
GO ON.

WE'RE NOT TALKING ABOUT JOY BUZZERS HERE. THAT'D REQUIRE SOME PRETTY HIGH-TECH STUFF.
MAYBE HE WAS JUST MAKING SURE IT WORKED BEFORE USING IT FOR WHAT HE'S *REALLY* GOT PLANNED.
THIS COULD BE JUST THE BEGINNING.

JESUS. I HOPE YOU'RE WRONG ABOUT THIS ONE, PARTNER.

"I *REALLY* HOPE YOU'RE WRONG."

HEAR ME, BROTHERS AND SISTERS. FOR ***FORTY YEARS*** THE LORD BADE HIS CHOSEN PEOPLE WANDER IN THE WILDERNESS, WHILE THE CANAANITES ***DEFILED*** THEIR PROMISED LAND.

BUT EVEN AS HE HUMBLED HIS CHILDREN, HE DID NOT FORGET! HE CAME TO THEM AS MANNA FROM HEAVEN, SUSTAINING THEM DURING THEIR AGE OF TRIAL.

AND WHEN THE TIME CAME FOR THEM TO TAKE THEIR PLACE IN THE LAND OF THEIR BIRTHRIGHT--

--THEIR WAY WAS PAVED WITH THE STONES OF RIGHTEOUSNESS.

SO IT WILL BE AGAIN.

"FOR I HAVE SEEN THE LORD'S WILL.
"THE HOUR IS SOON AT HAND WHEN HE WILL RAIN JUSTICE ON THE WICKED AND PROFANE.

LIKE EGYPT'S SONS, THEY WILL LEARN HE IS A GOD OF WRATH AS WELL AS LOVE.

"THOSE WHO HAVE PREPARED FOR HIM WITH FAITH AND OBEDIENCE, HE WILL WELCOME INTO THE LAND OF PLENTY.

WHILE THOSE WHO HAVE SCORNED HIM--
THOSE WHO HAVE CHOSEN THE PATH OF IDOLATRY, AVARICE, AND VANITY--

"--THEY WILL CRUMBLE AS WALLS BEFORE JOSHUA'S HORN.

THESE ARE THE WORDS OF THE LORD, AS SPOKEN UNTO ME.
HALLELUJAH AND AMEN.

NEWS RADIO, WGNU
HERE'S THE WORD ON TONIGHT'S WEATHER:

IT'S GOING TO BE A BALMY EVENING, WITH A LOW OF 86 AND A HIGH OF 92.

AND THOSE OF YOU WHO ENJOYED LAST NIGHT'S FIREWORKS ARE IN FOR A TREAT.

THE WEATHER SERVICE FORECASTS MORE SCATTERED FLASH STORMS THROUGHOUT THE NIGHT AND INTO THE EARLY MORNING.

SO IF YOU'RE VENTURING OUT, BE SURE TO USE THE SKYWALKS. YOU DON'T WANT TO GET CAUGHT OUTDOORS TONIGHT.
IT'S GOING TO BE ANOTHER ***WILD*** ONE.

Journal of Applied Cybernetics

January 2054

Paradise Found

Possibility and fulfillment in the age of the surrogate

by William Laslo, PhD

Without question, the most socially and economically significant technological event of the last quarter-century has been the invention of the surrogate. As this paper will show, never before in human history has the consumer been offered a product capable of delivering such dramatic personal change. The ramifications of the surrogate's rapid assimilation into everyday living can be witnessed in virtually every facet of culture, particularly in the United States where in the twenty years since their introduction the portion of the adult population that either owns or has operated a surrogate has risen to an astounding 92%. With surrogate technology in a constant state of refinement, there is no evidence to suggest this trend will be reversed. The improvements and transformations enjoyed by the operating public are here to stay, which leaves us with the question: What, if anything, remains to be overcome?

The sweeping changes that surrogates have affected on the American cultural landscape are due largely to the technology's secondary benefits, i.e., those benefits made apparent only after surrogates reached the marketplace and not during the conceptual and design stages.[1] It is largely because of these secondary benefits, however, that surrogates have enjoyed such widespread popularity with the consumer. While the list of secondary benefits is exhaustive—and perhaps better served in its entirety by a format larger than this paper—there are three areas in which surrogates have transformed American society with a scope so broad and an impact so profound as to be worthy of discussion in and of themselves.

"...the portion of the adult population that either owns or has operated a surrogate has risen to an astounding 92%."

They are race and gender relations, law enforcement and crime, and individual and public health.

I. Race and Gender Relations

In the United States, debates over race and gender equality have never been far removed from the public forum. At best these debates act as peaceful intellectual vehicles for the nurturing of the egalitarianism that has long been a hallmark of the nation, often prompting much needed legal reform.[2] At worst they degrade to violent protest, giving rise to such militant factions as the Black Panthers and Ku Klux Klan or culminating in disruptive displays of public upheaval akin to the New York-Philadelphia riots of 2026. No matter the tactic or strategy, however, it is an unfortunate truth that the differences between races and genders have remained largely unresolved.

The use of surrogates across demographic groups has opened a new approach to confronting inequality. Offering operators a certain measure of anonymity, surrogates render actual race and gender irrelevant and instead shift all demographic classifications to the implied race and gender of the surrogate unit being operated. The result is a cross-cultural condition of ambiguity, through which operators can remove race and gender considerations from their social interactions. When taking into account this function of ambiguity, it is logical to conclude that the proliferation of the surrogate in contemporary American culture would abolish such separatist philosophies as prejudice and stereotyping. It is interesting to note, however, that in some regards surrogates have only served to reinforce these discriminatory policies, often with interesting results.

Perhaps the most illustrative example is the treatment of gender discrimination in employer hiring practices. Paradoxically, by embracing the principles of gender stereotyping, operators can use gender-other units to increase workplace diversity and gain access to jobs they might otherwise be excluded from. A recent study of airline industry employees conducted by Pembroke College showed that those employed as skycaps, ticketing agents, and in-flight stewards were 37% more likely to operate a surrogate whose gender was consistent with the traditionally held view of their job, even if doing so required the purchasing of a gender-other unit. This trend increased dramatically for pilots, revealing 98% of female pilots questioned to be operators of gender-other units. When gender-other operators were asked about their motives, 82% cited a belief that gender-actual units posed an impediment to being hired.[3]

What this shows is the replacement of stereotyping as it is has been generally understood with a new, perceived stereotyping. Employers can use the demographic ambiguity offered by surrogates to uphold the staffing expectations of their customer base by allowing preconceptions to be formed not as a function of actual gender, but assumed gender. This new brand of stereotyping provides job seekers with access to careers and professional fields they might otherwise be barred from, and at the same time allows companies to maintain the business environment with which their customers are most comfortable, thereby insulating them from the adverse effects of hiring outside the bounds of tradition. Most importantly, it ensures that an applicant's skills and capabilities are the only criteria upon which an employer's hiring decisions are made, achieving a level of equality in the workplace that past strategies such as quotas and affirmative action strived for, but never fully attained.

Efforts to circumvent demographic classifications need not be so secretive to achieve a desired effect. Case in point is the 2042 state congressional race of Albert Coe in Detroit, Michigan. Caucasian by descent, Coe operated an African-American surrogate throughout his campaign to seek election in a predominantly black congressional district. Unlike the airline industry example cited above where an assumed condition replaced the operator's true condition in the public eye, Coe's race was widely publicized throughout his campaign. Touting his choice of surrogate as an illustration of his willingness to represent the constituency according to its best interests, regardless of racial differences, Coe was able to relate to the voter in a manner that would not have been possible without a surrogate. Though opposing candidates made attempts to discredit Coe, resulting in some of the most bitterly negative campaign advertisements in recent memory, Coe won the seat and became the district's first Caucasian representative in over thirty years.[4] Extrapolating this example further, it is not hard to envision the global impact of such a strategy in venues where racial divides often lessen the chances of productive interaction, foreign relations and international business being the two that come most immediately to mind.

II. Law Enforcement and Crime

Since their entry into American society began in the middle 2030s, surrogates have done more to reduce the crime rate and improve public safety than any other invention in this country's history. This can be credited to the fact that, while the focus of pre-surrogate legal reforms was to control crime through reactive measures such as stiffer penalties and mandatory sentencing, the post-surrogate world has become a more proactive one aimed at preventing crime rather than dealing with its aftermath. The most obvious change has been the movement from live-body to all-surrogate police forces, a practice first tested during the anti-surrogate riots of 2039 and adopted in precincts across the nation after its success. This strategy has lead to an increase in the number of law enforcement officers, while at the same time making the job of policing far less hazardous. It is more compelling, however, to consider the consequences of the surrogate presence during criminal situations, particularly in matters of violent crime. Such consideration leads to a new interpretation of perpetrator and victim.

While it is true that the majority of crimes are nonviolent—burglary, larceny, fraud—it is equally true that any discussion of crime and its control will culminate with a dialogue on violent crime, if for no other reason than it represents deviant behavior at its most brutal and devastating. It is fortunate, then, that it is with the second grouping that surrogates have achieved the most measurable results. Due to the unit/operator paradigm that substitutes the former for the latter in the natural world, crimes that once would have been considered violent are now being reclassified as little more than offenses against property.[5] Assaults, armed robberies, violent acts of passion—all of these crimes and many more have had their physical effects negated by the absence of live victims at the scene. Just as significantly, the mental trauma often endured by victims in the aftermath of violent episodes, such as that suffered by women following a rape or sexual assault, is no longer a factor because an operator can terminate their involvement in such events by removing the virtual reality device that links their mind to their unit's experience. Violence has been stripped of both its physical potency and its tragic legacy.

"...'dead men tell no tales' has lost its veracity, as the unit / operator paradigm ensures that for every crime there will be at least one surviving witness."

The substitution of the unit for the operator and the subsequent shift in classification from violent to property crime has had a domino effect, providing unanticipated solutions to some of the quandaries that have plagued the criminal justice system for decades. For example, overcrowding in the nation's penal institutions is virtually nonexistent today, due in large part to the fact that the majority of criminals are punished through courtroom litigation and monetary settlements. This reduction in prison populations has shifted the financial burden of punishment away from the state and federal governments that have historically shouldered it and toward the offender, who must produce compensation to injured parties for the damage they have caused. Unexpectedly, the possibility of costly litigation and a court-mandated property settlement is proving a better deterrent to crime than the threat of incarceration, as it seems would-be criminals deem financial hardship a worse penalty than imprisonment.

Just as great a deterrent to violent crime is the certainty of the eyewitness account. Experiencing the event, but not party to it, operators can offer investigators clues and testimony that would not be possible without the surrogate. The age-old criminal maxim "dead men tell no tales" has lost its veracity, as the unit/operator paradigm ensures that for every crime there will be at least one surviving witness. With the introduction of new technology that grants operators the ability to record the data transmitted by their units, the reliability of eyewitness accounts will be strengthened, providing law enforcement with reenactments of crimes and images of perpetrators untainted by bias or memory. As research and development brings further advances, the task of apprehending and prosecuting offenders will be made even easier, and perhaps, for the first time in history, crime truly will not pay.

III. Individual and Public Health

For a thorough understanding of how deeply surrogate technology is changing the face of society one must look to the issues of individual and public health. Rather than detail the myriad of improvements surrogates have exacted on the American healthcare front, affecting everything from carpal tunnel syndrome to the common cold, it is instructive to focus on a single health issue, and then use the discussion as a model from which to draw conclusions about the technology's impact on the broader field.

By 2030, the tobacco industry boasted a consumer base larger than at any other time in its existence. Along with the record profits enjoyed by the industry's leading producers came an increase in the incidence of tobacco-related illnesses, placing measurable strain on a healthcare infrastructure struggling to cope with the legacy of addiction and abuse. Patients suffering from such ailments as emphysema, heart disease, and lung and throat cancers entered hospitals and medical offices at a rate faster than staff, research, and funding could offer treatment.

Regrettably, for many of those patients the die had already been cast, but for future generations there came a panacea. Surrogates provided a solution by rendering the problem irrelevant. Capable of delivering a distilled experience consisting solely of stimuli, surrogates transmit sensory data via the virtual reality link to the operator's brain where the appropriate response is elicited. Using the act of smoking as an example, as an operator's brain directs their unit to inhale tobacco smoke, the sensory input associated with the experience (taste, sight, and smell sensations, as well as momentary euphoria and satisfaction of the oral fixation) are returned to the operator's brain to be interpreted as stimuli. All other physiological effects (lung damage, constriction of the arteries, increased risk of applicable cancers) become inconsequential, as it is only the mind that experiences the act and not the body.

The results have been substantial. As statistics are beginning to show, while the past ten years have seen a steady climb in the number of smokers in America, the number of newly reported cases of smoking-related illnesses has declined. By stepping between the operator and the physical world, surrogates have broken the causal connection that exists between smoking and disease, allowing both big tobacco and healthcare to benefit from the common ground afforded by the technology.[6] Given the cumulative nature of these illnesses and their propensity to increase in severity and number over time, it can only be assumed that the trend will continue, and that with each new generation born into this culture of experience without consequence will come a greater disparity between the number of people who smoke and the number who suffer.

Having already considered the issue of smoking, drug and alcohol use and their adverse effects are the health crises one most immediately recognizes as affected, and it is true that surrogates have made these formerly hazardous activities safe for operators.[7] The true breadth of the technology's impact on individual and public health becomes apparent, however, when the paradigm is applied across an even wider spectrum. Debilitating conditions such as arthritis, fibromyalgia, and muscular dystrophy have been curtailed in their effect, allowing the afflicted to live normal lives through surrogate bodies. Communicable diseases are particularly susceptible to the technology's influence, though we will not enjoy the greatest rewards until surrogates have saturated the international marketplace to the degree that they have domestically. While all of the health concerns discussed above are high-profile in nature, it would be remiss to ignore the more garden-variety accidents, ailments, and injuries suffered by millions every day, the reduction of which translates into an improved quality of life for all.

Notes

1 Dr. Michael Kreider, a member of the original surrogate creative team, had this to say about the early days of design: "When we were in the labs developing the software and production standards, our goal was to provide the physically handicapped with a prosthetic means to overcome their disabilities. It wasn't until surrogates reached the public and we saw who was buying them and what they were being used for that we began to understand the wider range of possibilities and how restrictive our intentions had been." (Nathan Horowitz, "Interview With a Pioneer," Popular Robotics, February 2047, p. 62).

2 The Equal Rights Amendment to the Constitution and the Supreme Court decision in Brown vs. Board of Education are two examples of such reform.

3 It is important to note that employers, in accordance with the full disclosure laws that govern application processes, are aware of each applicant's true gender, but view the willingness to work in gender-other scenarios as a positive sign that the applicant prioritizes the employer's public image above their own.

4 For a compete account of Coe's landmark campaign see John Wharton's "Under the Skin: Politics and the Dawn of the Anyman."

5 This argument applies to crimes committed outside the home. As critics are quick to point out, surrogates have had a lesser effect on curbing the incidence of violent crime inside the home. Acts of domestic violence are no less devastating for their location, it is certain, but the impact of the technology on violent crimes committed outside the home is significant and merits its own discussion.

6 Indeed, the formerly antithetical aims of big tobacco and healthcare have now brought the industries together and resulted in several joint ventures, including an advertising campaign that admonishes would-be tobacco users to "Smoke responsibly: Operating surrogates = optimum health."

7 It is also worth noting that surrogates, for reasons discussed in Part II of this essay, have virtually eliminated tragedies such as DUI fatalities and drug-related murders, revealing the extent to which the application of the technology in a single area can impact seemingly unrelated fields.

chapter
TWO

Life Unfiltered

MAY 9, 2054.
CLARK TECHNOLOGIES
CGM
CGM

YOU KEEP CALLING ME IN LIKE THIS, PETE, AND I'LL START TO THINK YOU'RE SWEET ON ME.

DON'T FLATTER YOURSELF.
WE'VE GOT TWO MORE FRYJOBS, ONE REGISTERED TO A JOHN R. CROWLEY, AND THE OTHER TO A MARQUES P. CULBERTSON--TWO OF CLARK TECH'S FINEST.
POLICE LINE DO NOT CROSS POLICE LINE DO NOT CROSS

ARE WE STILL LOOKING FOR THE LIGHT SWITCH?
METRO POWER'S TOPSIDE WORKING ON IT, BUT IT'LL BE A FEW MINUTES. THEY HAD TO INSTALL A NEW TRANSFORMER UNIT.
JOHN

LET ME GUESS . . . THE WIRING ON THE OLD ONE WAS FUSED TOGETHER, LIKE WOULD HAPPEN IF IT WAS--OH, I DON'T KNOW--HIT BY LIGHTNING MAYBE?
GEE, HARV. HOW'D YOU KNOW?

I'M A NATURAL. I MAY BE GOING OUT ON A LIMB HERE, BUT I DON'T THINK IT WAS LIGHTNING THAT GOT TO THESE TWO.
BEING INDOORS KIND OF RULES THAT OUT, DOESN'T IT. YOU THINKING WHAT I'M THINKING?

YEAH. IT'S DEJA VU ALL OVER AGAIN.

AT APPROXIMATELY 10:30 P.M., ELECTRICAL POWER TO THE ENTIRE COMPLEX IS INTERRUPTED, TRIPPING THE ALARM AND SENDING AN ALERT TO OFF-SITE SECURITY.

A FLASH STORM IS MOVING OVER THE AREA, SO CULBERTSON FOLLOWS PROCEDURE--THAT'S THE PROTOCOL MANUAL HE'S FACEDOWN ON--AND CALLS TO INFORM SECURITY THE OUTAGE IS WEATHER-RELATED.

THE OPERATOR LOGS THE TRANSMISSION AT 10:36, MUTES THE ALARM, AND TELLS THE RESPONSE TEAM TO STAND DOWN.

SO OUR ELUSIVE MAN IN BLACK PROVIDED THE LIGHTNING TO THE BUILDING'S TRANSFORMER UNIT--

--AND THEN BROKE IN THROUGH THE VENTILATION SHAFT, USING THE SOUND OF THE ALARM TO MASK HIS ENTRY.
THAT'S MY THEORY.

WELL, HE'S GOT GUTS. I'VE NEVER SEEN A PERP *INTENTIONALLY* SET AN ALARM DURING A BREAK-IN.

NEXT HE DISABLES THE BACKUP GENERATOR THAT CONTINUES TO POWER THE SECURITY CAMERAS DURING AN OUTAGE, TAKING AWAY THE GUARDS' ABILITY TO MONITOR THE PREMISES FROM THESE SCREENS.

USING THE DARKNESS TO HIS ADVANTAGE, HE APPROACHES CULBERTSON FROM BEHIND AND ZAPS HIM IN HIS CHAIR.

CROWLEY IS STANDING A FEW FEET AWAY, AND HE GETS OFF A SINGLE ROUND FROM HIS SIDEARM --A STANDARD ISSUE SONIC GUN--BEFORE HE'S LIKEWISE OVERCOME.

THESE BURNS INDICATE POINT OF CONTACT WAS THE TEMPLES.
CULBERTSON HAS SIMILAR MARKS UNDER EACH ARM.

HERE'S THE SHELL CASING FROM CROWLEY'S ROUND. SINCE OUR GUY KEPT COMING WE CAN ASSUME THE SHOT MISSED, BUT THERE'S NO SIGN OF THE SCREAMER DART.
IT COULD'VE RICOCHETED AND ENDED UP ANYWHERE.

AND THAT'S THAT. WITH THE GUARDS TAKEN CARE OF, HE HAD PLENTY OF TIME TO GET WHAT HE CAME FOR.
IF OFF-SITE SECURITY HADN'T ATTEMPTED A FOLLOW-UP CALL AT 11:00, WE STILL WOULDN'T KNOW ANYTHING HAD HAPPENED.

LET THERE BE LIGHT.
DETECTIVES?

HARVEY, THIS IS DR. HOFFMAN. HE'S CLARK TECH'S ON-CALL STAFF MEMBER FOR THE EVENING.
DOC, THIS IS MY PARTNER, LIEUTENANT GREER.
SORRY TO GET YOU UP AT THIS HOUR, DOC.
IT COMES WITH THE TERRITORY. IF YOU'LL FOLLOW ME, I THINK I'VE FOUND WHAT WAS TAKEN.

THIS IS ONE OF OUR RESEARCH AND DEVELOPMENT LABS. WE USE IT TO CONDUCT TRIALS ON NEW PROCESSOR CHIPS.

WE STORE THE CHIPS UNDERGOING TESTING IN THIS CONTAINER.

LOT 1006 IS MISSING.

WHAT'S LOT 1006?
WE'VE BEEN DEVELOPING AN EMP DELIVERY SYSTEM THAT WOULD ALLOW THE TARGETING OF SPECIFIC FREQUENCY RANGES. LOT 1006 IS THE FIRST PROCESSOR TO SHOW ANY REAL PROMISE.

MY PARTNER MISSED THE DAY WE LEARNED ABOUT THIS IN THE ACADEMY, DOC, SO WHY DON'T YOU EXPLAIN WHAT AN E-M-P IS.

ELECTRO-MAGNETIC PULSE. IT'S A BURST OF ENERGY THAT DISRUPTS ELECTRONIC CIRCUITS WITHOUT DAMAGING PEOPLE OR STRUCTURES.
THE PROBLEM IS THEY'RE INDISCRIMINATE. THEY AFFECT A WIDE RANGE OF FREQUENCIES, SO ONE BURST DISRUPTS ALL OF THE CIRCUITRY INSIDE THE PULSE'S RADIUS. LOT 1006 IS A STEP IN OVERCOMING THAT.

BUT WHAT WOULD SOMEONE WANT WITH THE CHIP? IT'S USELESS WITHOUT THE COMPATIBLE SOFTWARE.
AND WHERE WOULD YOU FIND THAT?

ONE OF OUR SUBSIDIARY COMPANIES, CDV LABORATORIES, HAS A TRIAL VERSION, BUT THEY HAVEN'T WORKED OUT ALL OF THE BUGS YET.
OKAY. THANKS, DOC. WE'RE GOING TO LOOK AROUND FOR A MINUTE.
TAKE YOUR TIME, DETECTIVES.

HOW MANY WEDGIES YOU FIGURE A SCIENCE GEEK HAS TO GET BEFORE HE BUYS A SURRIE *THAT* BIG?
AT LEAST ONE TOO MANY.
THERE WERE A LOT OF GIZMOS IN THAT CONTAINER, BUT OUR GUY WAS IN AND OUT PRETTY QUICK. I'D SAY HE KNEW WHAT HE WAS AFTER.

THIS PLACE MIGHT NOT HAVE THE BEST SECURITY, BUT IT'S COMPETENT ENOUGH. HE TOOK IT APART LIKE IT WAS A POWDERPUFF FOOTBALL TEAM.
YEAH. LOOKS LIKE HE HAD A PEEK AT THE PLAYBOOK.

SOUNDS LIKE AN INSIDE JOB.
COULD BE. PUT SOME OF THE OTHER GUYS ON IT. THEY'LL LOVE THE OVERTIME.

WHAT ARE WE GOING TO DO?
STARTING TOMORROW NIGHT, WE'LL BE SITTING ON CDV LABS.

YOU THINK THAT'S HIS NEXT MOVE?
IF A GUY STEALS SOMETHING LIKE THIS, IT'S BECAUSE HE ALREADY HAS PLANS FOR IT.
THE DOC SAID HE'D NEED WHATEVER THEY'VE GOT AT CDV, SO THAT'S WHERE WE'LL WAIT.

GET SOME SLEEP, PARTNER. WE'VE GOT LONG NIGHTS AHEAD OF US.
YOU TAKE THE CAR. I THINK BETTER ON THE TUBES.

SMASH

--NEAREST BUILDING . . . EMERGENCY STOP. PLEASE PROCEED CAREFULLY TO THE NEAREST BUILDING . . . EMERGENCY STOP. PLEASE PROCEED CAREFULLY--

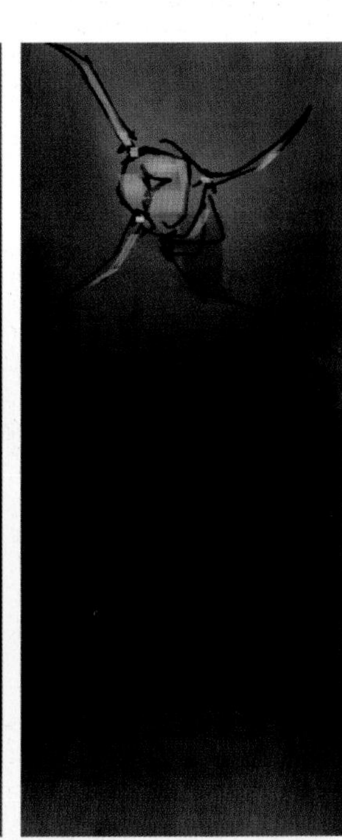

AAAA!!!

IT'S NOT THAT BAD, LIEUTENANT. PAIN NEVER HURTS AS MUCH WHEN YOU KNOW NO DAMAGE IS DONE.

ISN'T IT STRANGE HOW THE THINGS WE LOOK FOR OFTEN FIND US WHEN WE LEAST EXPECT THEM?
WHAT DO YOU WANT?

WHEN I WAS A CHILD, MY FATHER HAD A PHOTOGRAPH OF ELEVEN MEN SITTING ON A STEEL GIRDER.
THESE MEN--THE STEEPLEJACKS AS THEY WERE CALLED--WERE HUNDREDS OF FEET IN THE AIR, EATING LUNCH ON THE SKELETON OF ROCKEFELLER CENTER.

I WAS IN AWE OF THEM. THAT THEY COULD DINE SO CLOSE TO DEATH . . .
THE STRANGE MIXTURE OF FEAR AND EXHILARATION THAT MUST'VE MADE THEM FEEL SO INCREDIBLY ***ALIVE***.

NOW HERE YOU ARE, FIFTEEN STORIES ABOVE THE GROUND, AND WHAT DO YOU FEEL?
NOTHING. YOU FEEL NO FEAR, NO EXHILARATION. YOU CERTAINLY DON'T FEEL ALIVE.

BECAUSE YOU ***AREN'T*** HERE. YOU HAVE TRADED FLESH AND BONE FOR COSMETICS AND ALLOY.
YOU LIVE A FILTERED LIFE.

YOU ASKED WHAT I WANT?
EVERYONE DREAMS OF CHANGING THE WORLD. I ONLY WANT TO CHANGE IT BACK.
WAIT--

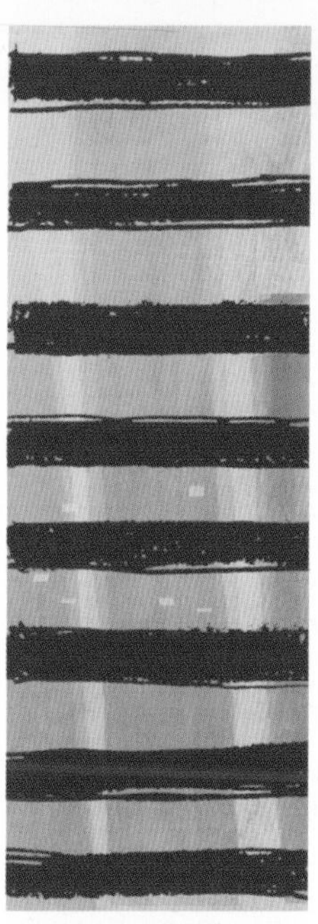
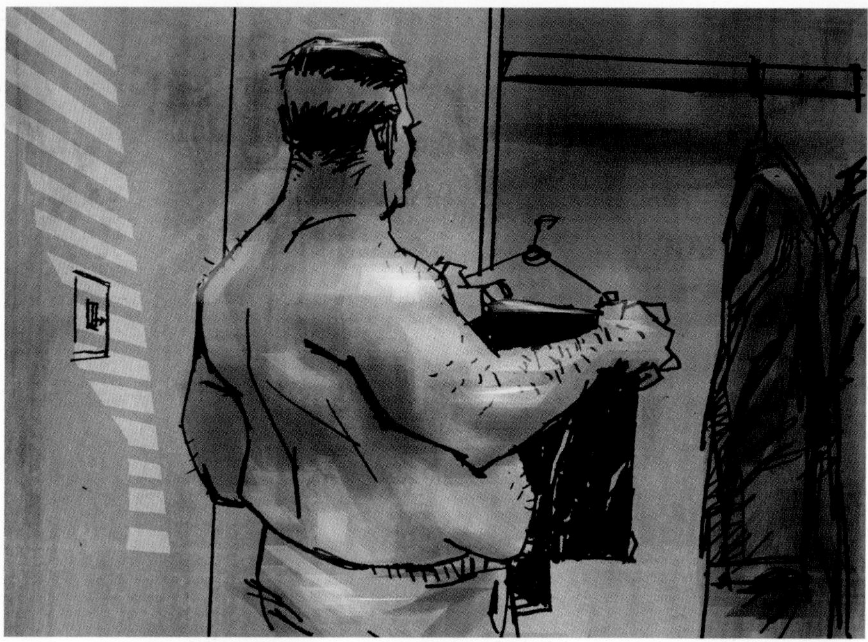
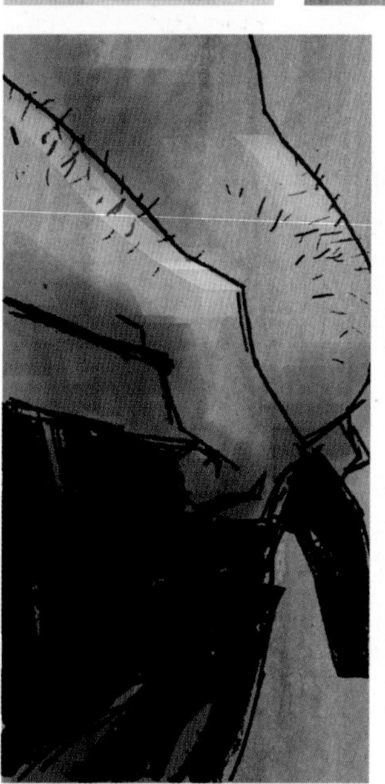

DISPATCH? THIS IS LIEUTENANT GREER.

YES.
NO.
EVERYTHING'S FINE.

CONTACT SERGEANT FORD AND HAVE HIM MEET ME AT THE PRECINCT.

JESUS, HARV. IT'S YOU. I MEAN *REALLY* YOU.
IN THE FLESH. SHUT THE DOOR.

I HAVEN'T SEEN YOU SINCE . . . HELL, I DON'T KNOW WHEN. YOU'RE A LITTLE THINNER ON TOP.
NICE OF YOU TO NOTICE.

SCREWS SAID YOUR SURRIE SUFFERED SOME PRETTY BAD IMPACT DAMAGE, BUT IT'S NOTHING THAT CAN'T BE FIXED. IN THE MEANTIME, THERE'S A TEMP WAITING FOR YOU AT THE DEPARTMENT POOL.
NO THANKS. I'M GOING TO WORK THIS ONE LIVE AND IN COLOR.

YOU'RE JOKING.
'FRAID NOT. YOU NEVER GET THE URGE TO SEE IF YOU'RE STILL UP TO THE JOB?

WHO'D SMOKE MY CIGARETTES FOR ME? BESIDES, THIS CASE ISN'T THE TYPE TO MAKE ME PRESS MY LUCK. WE'RE CHASING A REAL NUTJOB HERE.

MAYBE SO, BUT IT ISN'T PEOPLE HE HAS A PROBLEM WITH. IT'S SURRIES.
AND I THINK I KNOW WHO HE'S WORKING FOR.
WHO?

AN OLD ACQUAINTANCE.
RING
ZAIRE POWELL III
ALIAS "THE PROPHET"

YOU KNOW THE PROPHET?
I WAS A BEAT COP WHEN THE RIOTS OF '39 BROKE OUT. THE DEPARTMENT MOVED ME TO RIOT SQUAD UNTIL THE ACCORD WAS SIGNED.

I NEVER MET HIM, BUT I SAT THROUGH ENOUGH BRIEFINGS TO UNDERSTAND HIM, AND I THINK HE AND STEEPLEJACK HAVE A LOT IN COMMON. MAYBE TOO MUCH.
STEEPLEJACK?

WE'VE GOT TO CALL OUR GUY SOMETHING.
WHY THAT?

BECAUSE HE HAS AN AFFINITY FOR THE OLD-TIME STEELWORKERS.
HE TOLD ME ALL ABOUT IT RIGHT BEFORE HE PITCHED ME OFF THE SKYWALK.

I GUESS THAT EXPLAINS HIS SWINGING FROM THE ROOFTOPS.
A MEANS OF TRAVEL OUR DEPARTMENT IS WOEFULLY ILL-EQUIPPED TO DEAL WITH. HE'S SMART. YOU'VE GOT TO GIVE HIM THAT MUCH.

UNTIL HE CAME AFTER YOU, WE DIDN'T KNOW A THING ABOUT HIM. IF HE'S SO SMART, WHY'D HE TIP HIS HAND?
BECAUSE HE THINKS WE CAN'T STOP HIM.
HE MIGHT BE RIGHT.

WE'LL SEE. SO, YOU THINK THE PROPHET AND THIS STEEPLECHASE--
JACK. STEEPLEJACK.

STEEPLEJACK. YOU THINK THEY'RE SOMEHOW CONNECTED?
HE WAS QUOTING THE PROPHET'S BRAND OF ANTI-SURROGATE RHETORIC, THAT'S FOR SURE.

AND THAT EMP CHIP SOUNDS LIKE THE PERFECT WAY TO DESTROY SURRIES IN BIG NUMBERS.
WHICH IS EXACTLY WHAT THE PROPHET'S BEEN HOPING FOR.

SO WE'RE RIDING DOWN TO THE REZ, WHERE THE PROPHET IS GOING TO ADMIT HE'S PLANNING A LARGE-SCALE ATTACK ON THE CITY, GIVING US ALL THE EXCUSE WE NEED TO WIPE HIS LITTLE KINGDOM OFF THE MAP.
NOT VERY LIKELY.

THEN WHY NOT PUT IT IN A LETTER AND SAVE THE TRIP?
THE PROPHET'S EGO IS HIS WEAKNESS. IF I'M IN HIS TERRITORY, HE WON'T MISS THE CHANCE TO GLOAT.

WHAT IF HE DOESN'T LET US IN?
YOU, HE WON'T. HE DOESN'T DEAL WITH SURROGATES.
BUT HE'LL LET ME IN. HE CAN'T AFFORD TO LOSE FACE IN FRONT OF HIS PEOPLE.

DREAD
RESERVATION

NICE OF THEM TO HAVE A WELCOMING COMMITTEE.

I NEED TO SEE THE PROPHET.

THAT BADGE IS WORTH ABOUT AS MUCH AS YOUR *LAWS* OUT HERE, POLICEMAN.
AND THE PROPHET DON'T SIT DOWN WITH *ABOMINATIONS*.

I WOULDN'T DREAM OF OFFENDING HIS DELICATE SENSIBLITIES. I CAME TO SPEAK WITH HIM MAN TO MAN.
THAT SO?

LET'S JUST SEE.
BACK AWAY!

WHAT YOU GOT, COP? A SONIC GUN? THAT'LL GIVE ME A *REAL* NASTY HEADACHE.
BUT IF YOUR FRIEND HERE IS AS REAL AS HE SAYS HE IS, WHO YOU THINK'S GONNA END UP *WORSE*?

IT'S ALRIGHT, PETE.
YEAH, IT'S *ALRIGHT*.

WELL LOOKIT THAT . . .

ADMIT THE VISITOR.

THE PROPHET HAS AGREED TO SPEAK WITH HIM.

LUTHER WILL TAKE YOU TO HIM.
BUT THE ABOMINATION STAYS.

I WILL SEND FOR YOU WHEN WE ARE FINISHED, BROTHER LUTHER.

MY PARTNER THOUGHT YOU WOULDN'T ADMIT ME.
IF A SHEPHERD HAS A HUNDRED SHEEP, AND ONE OF THEM STRAYS, IS HE NOT MORE DELIGHTED OVER THAT ONE SHEEP WHEN IT RETURNS THAN OVER THE NINETY-NINE THAT DID NOT STRAY?

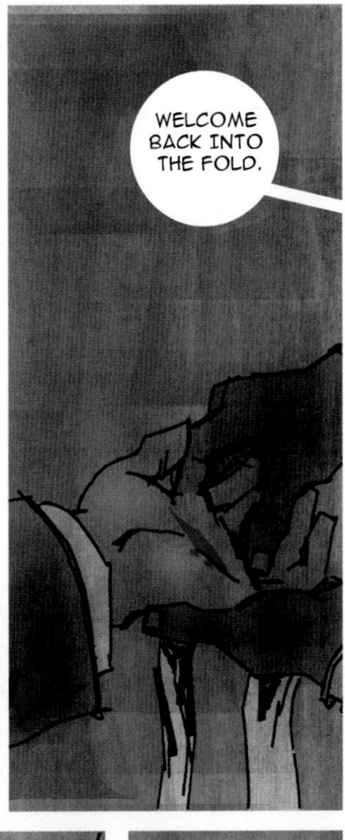
WELCOME BACK INTO THE FOLD.

I KNEW YOU WOULDN'T MEET WITH ME OTHERWISE.
I THINK THERE IS MORE TO IT THAN THAT, DON'T YOU, OFFICER?

IT'S ***LIEUTENANT.*** AND DON'T GO CELEBRATING JUST YET.
THESE PEOPLE MAY HAVE FOUND A PROPHET, BUT ALL I SEE IS ZAIRE POWELL III, MURDERER AND CON MAN.
IF YOUR EYE CAUSES YOUR DOWNFALL, THEN TEAR IT OUT AND FLING IT AWAY. IT IS BETTER TO LIVE WITH ONE EYE THAN TO KEEP BOTH AND BE CAST INTO THE FIRES OF HELL.

NOW WHAT DO YOU WISH TO SPEAK ABOUT?

THERE'S BEEN A SERIES OF CRIMES IN THE CITY.
AND YOU BELIEVE I HAVE CAUSED THEM?

THE SIMILARITY BETWEEN THEIR ANTI-SURROGATE NATURE AND YOUR OWN WELL-KNOWN AGENDA *IS* UNCANNY.

I AM MERELY A SEER AND COMMUNICATOR OF GOD'S WILL, NOT AN INSTRUMENT OF IT. PHYSICAL ACTION IS THE PROVIDENCE OF OTHER MEN.

FUNNY, I DON'T REMEMBER YOU HAVING THAT POLICY FIFTEEN YEARS AGO WHEN YOU INCITED YOUR FOLLOWERS TO RIOT.
TIME IS A SOFTER JUDGE THAN MEN, LIEUTENANT. YOU WILL FIND THAT NOW MY PEOPLE UNDERSTAND ME TO BE A PROPONENT OF PEACE AND LOVE.

IN OTHER WORDS, YOU'VE LEARNED YOU CAN'T CONQUER THE CITY BY FORCE AND HAVE DECIDED TO CHANGE YOUR TUNE.

THERE ARE NONE SO BLIND AS THOSE WHO WILL NOT SEE.

WHY IS IT SO HARD FOR YOU TO BELIEVE THAT THE LORD WILL PUNISH THOSE WHO BLASPHEME HIS NAME?

HOW LONG DO YOU THINK HE WILL ALLOW YOUR HEATHENISH WAYS? EACH OF US IS MADE IN GOD'S PERFECT IMAGE--

--AND YET YOU WOULD SEEK TO IMPROVE UPON THAT PERFECTION. TO CREATE AN EXISTENCE JUDGED NOT BY THE LAWS OF GOD BUT MEN.

WHEN THE EGYPTIANS REFUSED TO HEED GOD'S WORD, DID HE NOT SEND AN ANGEL OF DEATH TO SMITE THEM?

WHY SHOULD IT BE ANY DIFFERENT FOR YOUR NATION?

THESE RECENT ATTACKS ARE JEOPARDIZING THE AGREEMENT THAT PROTECTS YOU AND YOUR PEOPLE, POWELL.

IF I FIND YOU'RE BEHIND THEM, NO AMOUNT OF SERMONIZING WILL KEEP ME FROM DRAGGING YOU OUT OF HERE IN HANDCUFFS.

PREPARE YOURSELF, LIEUTENANT. THE DAY OF THE LORD IS COMING LIKE A THIEF IN THE NIGHT.

"WHAT WILL BE THE JUDGMENT OF YOU AND YOURS?"

WHAT HAPPENED TO YOUR HAND?

IT'S NOTHING.

IT HAPPENED AT WORK, DIDN'T IT? IT'S THAT CASE YOU'RE WORKING ON.

IT'S JUST A SCRATCH, MARGARET. IT'S FINE.
JUST A SCRATCH **THIS** TIME. I WANT YOU TO GET A REPLACEMENT UNIT TOMORROW.

NO. I HAVE TO WORK THIS CASE THE WAY I THINK IS BEST.
WHAT HAPPENS IF YOU **REALLY** GET HURT? OR **KILLED**? THERE'S A **REASON** THE DEPARTMENT HAS A SURROGATE POOL IN RESERVE.

YOU'RE BEING EXTREME. NOTHING'S GOING TO HAPPEN.
I'M BEING EXTREME?

YES, YOU'RE BEING EXTREME. ABOUT INSISTING ON SEPARATE BEDROOMS, AND SENDING YOUR SURROGATE TO DINNER--

--AND STAYING BOTTLED UP IN YOUR ROOM ALL DAY, EVERY DAY. CHRIST, MARGARET, I DON'T EVEN KNOW WHAT YOU LOOK LIKE ANYMORE.

THIS IS WHAT I LOOK LIKE. YOUNG. ATTRACTIVE.

AND WHAT IF I DON'T LIKE IT?

IT MUST BE NICE TO BE YOU, HARVEY--

--TO NOT CARE THAT YOU'VE PUT ON WEIGHT AND GOTTEN OLDER. I'M SORRY TO DISAPPOINT YOU, BUT I DON'T SHARE YOUR SELF-CONFIDENCE.

IT'S NOT SELF-CONFIDENCE, IT'S ***REALITY***. THIS IS WHO I AM, AND LINKING DOESN'T CHANGE THAT.

SPEAK FOR YOURSELF. WHEN I'M LINKED, I LOOK YOUNGER. I ***FEEL*** YOUNGER. IF THAT'S NOT REALITY, I DON'T KNOW WHAT IS.

MARGARET, YOU'RE NOT THIRTY. YOU DON'T LOOK THE SAME AS WHEN WE GOT MARRIED, AND THAT'S OKAY. IT DOESN'T BOTHER ME.

WHAT A RELIEF! THIS MAY COME AS A ***SHOCK*** TO YOU, HARVEY, BUT YOUR OPINION DOESN'T MATTER TO ME.

MY REASONS FOR LINKING HAVE ***NOTHING*** TO DO WITH YOU!

HOME FIRES
BURNING

ABOVE THE FOLD,
GNN-TV

Aired November 23, 2013

WALKER PIERCE (Voice-over): They are events not easily forgotten: a palatial estate in the suburbs of Atlanta reduced in minutes to embers and debris.

UNIDENTIFIED MAN: I live twelve blocks over, but you could see the glow of the fire from my backyard. The smell of smoke hung in the air for days.

PIERCE (Voice-over): Scorched earth, charred furniture, photo albums and family keepsakes turned to ash. Worse yet were the bodies of the family that once lived inside: Zaire Powell Jr., a devoted father and respected businessman; Natalie Powell, a loving mother and active member in the church and community; and Kenyatta Powell, an infant who would never be old enough to remember the parents who loved her.

Natalie Powell's sister, Bernice Malloy, remembers that night all too well.

PIERCE: What was it like, having the police come to your door in the middle of the night and tell you what had occurred?

BERNICE MALLOY: You can't imagine. I asked them if they needed me to identify my sister's remains, and they told me there was nothing left to identify.

PIERCE (Voice-over): A family well-known in the most elite social circles, now burned so badly as to be unrecognizable to those who knew them best. As a community searched for answers, they were found in the most horrifying of places. Arrested and charged with arson and murder was Zaire Powell III, the thirteen-year-old boy who was the only surviving member of the family.

(MORE)

(CONT'D)

PIERCE: It must've been a tremendous shock when they took your nephew into custody. What were you thinking?

MALLOY: The same thing that I think to this day: There's no way that boy started that fire. I know him. I watched him grow. He's just not capable of something like that.

PIERCE (Voice-over): Though her only sister was gone, this would not signify the end for Bernice Malloy, but rather a new beginning. As the community sought to punish the boy they held responsible, Malloy began a crusade to save the only family she had left.

It would be a long and protracted battle, one that would pit her against the efforts of this man, Assistant District Attorney Joseph Caprice.

JOSEPH CAPRICE: Prosecuting a case like this is always difficult. The crime is so incomprehensible. It's only natural that Ms. Malloy would see innocence in her own flesh and blood because for her the alternative is unimaginable. But the evidence against Zaire Powell III was and is damning.

PIERCE: How so? There are stories in the news all the time about innocent people being wrongly accused--sometimes even wrongly convicted--of crimes they didn't commit. Can you say beyond a reasonable doubt that Zaire Powell started the fire?

CAPRICE: Beyond a reasonable doubt.

PIERCE: What makes you so sure?

CAPRICE: For one thing, the arson investigators concluded that the fire began inside the house, but there was no sign of forced entry. Second, testing concluded that the accelerant used to start the fire was of the same octane and had the same chemical additives as gasoline found in the gardener's shed, where, again, there was no sign of forced entry. So we knew the fire was started by someone with access to both locations. Only three people had that kind of access. Two of them died in the fire. The third is on trial for their murder.

PIERCE: So what do you say to a woman like Bernice Malloy, who insists on Powell's innocence? It can be argued that her personal relationship with the boy puts her in a better position to judge whether he is even capable of something like this.

CAPRICE: I would say to Bernice Malloy that the facts are the facts, and they don't lie.

PIERCE (Voice-over): Facts entered as evidence, the cornerstone of the criminal justice system. But to some they are not always so cut and dried.

MALLOY: The facts don't lie, but they don't always say what we think they do either. Who else had access to the house? How many gas stations sell the same gas?

PIERCE (Voice-over): But as the investigation continued, the

(MORE)

(CONT'D)

case against Malloy's nephew grew stronger. Digging through the rubble of the Powell home, investigators unearthed a motive even more unthinkable than the crime itself.

PIERCE: Were autopsies performed on the victims?

CAPRICE: The fire was started in the parents' bedroom, so their bodies were burned to a point where there wasn't much the medical examiners could do. But the body of the infant girl was more intact.

PIERCE: After examining her remains, what did the medical examiners conclude?

CAPRICE: Her lungs showed no signs of smoke inhalation.

PIERCE: Meaning what?

CAPRICE: She was already dead before the fire was started.

PIERCE (Voice-over): For Caprice and the investigators, the events of that deadly night were taking shape. The evidence suggested that the adolescent Powell had smothered his own sister and then set the blaze to cover up his crime. For Bernice Malloy, the news was devastating.

PIERCE: What went through your mind when the police told you how Kenyatta had died?

MALLOY: The grief was overwhelming. She was such a beautiful little girl. Who would do such a thing? But the police still haven't convinced me that Zaire was responsible. He wouldn't do that to his own family. He couldn't. They'll never make me believe otherwise.

PIERCE (Voice-over): Unfortunately for Malloy and her nephew, a jury would find the prosecution's case much more convincing. After only two days of deliberations, they rendered their verdict. They found Powell guilty of arson and three counts of murder.

PIERCE: When the foreman read the verdict, what was your reaction?

MALLOY: Sorrow. Frustration.

PIERCE: But you didn't stop fighting, did you?

MALLOY: You never stop fighting for your family.

PIERCE (Voice-over): So Brenda Malloy focused her efforts on the sentencing phase of the trial in a last, desperate attempt to help the young Powell. Opposing her once again was Joseph Caprice.

PIERCE: Though thirteen years of age, you asked the court to sentence Powell as an adult. Why?

CAPRICE: Powell is young in age, but not in mind. His plan was a careful one, and he executed it with a level of calm you would find in a career felon. It angered him that he wound up getting caught, but he showed no remorse. He knew what he had done was against the law. He just didn't think it was wrong.

(MORE)

(CONT'D)

PIERCE: But he's in the eighth grade. He watches cartoons and races remote-controlled cars. That doesn't sound like an adult.

CAPRICE: Under certain criteria, when the crime is heinous enough and the perpetrator is competent enough to understand the effects of his actions, the courts have found that it serves the public interest to sentence juveniles as adults. By smothering his infant sister and setting a fire to hide his crime, by acting with malice and forethought, Zaire Powell met those criteria.

PIERCE (Voice-over): Caprice asked the jury to sentence Powell to a term of life without parole. When they returned with their decision, both Caprice and Malloy were surprised by what they heard. Powell was sentenced to life in prison, but he would be eligible for parole in twenty-five years.

PIERCE: Was it any consolation to you when the jury announced its sentence?

MALLOY: You pray that people will see what you see, a happy child who loved his family and would never hurt them. I think the jury saw a glimpse of that, and I'm thankful for it. My nephew doesn't belong in jail, but I can accept that sometimes the Lord has plans for us that we don't always understand. There's a chance that someday we'll be able to sit together without cameras watching or barriers between us, and that chance, no matter how far away, is better than no chance at all.

PIERCE: Zaire Powell III began his term of incarceration in October. By the time he is eligible for parole, he will be thirty-eight years old. His lawyers are hard at work preparing their appeal. Brenda Malloy visits her nephew every Sunday.

(END)

chapter
THREE

Revelations

YOU HAVE A CALL.

YOU HAVE A CALL.

GREER.

WHERE ARE YOU, PETE? WE NEED TO BE BACK AT CDV BY--

ALRIGHT. LET ME GET THE SET ON.

GNN? YEAH, I GOT IT. WHAT'S SO IMPORT--

OH, CHRIST.
I'M DONNA REID WITH GNN HEADLINE NEWS--

MAY 12, 2054.

--AND TODAY I'M WITH ZAIRE POWELL III, KNOWN TO MANY AS SIMPLY ***THE PROPHET***, AT HIS HOME IN THE HEART OF DREAD RESERVATION.

IT HAS BEEN JUST UNDER ***FIFTEEN*** YEARS SINCE MR. POWELL'S LAST TELEVISED APPEARANCE.

IT WAS THEN THAT THE ACCORD BETWEEN HIMSELF AND THE GOVERNMENT OF CENTRAL GEORGIA METROPOLIS WAS RATIFIED, BRINGING AN END TO THE INFAMOUS ANTI-SURROGATE RIOTS OF 2039.

BUT TODAY, WITH THIS ***LIVE*** INTERVIEW, MR. POWELL'S LONG YEARS OF SILENCE ARE BROKEN.

MR. POWELL, THANK YOU FOR SPEAKING WITH US TODAY.
THREE DAYS AGO YOU WERE PAID A VISIT BY A LIEUTENANT IN THE METRO POLICE DEPARTMENT. PLEASE TELL US THE NATURE OF THAT VISIT.
YOU'D BETTER GET DOWN HERE. AND DON'T TALK TO ***ANYONE***.

LIEUTENANT HARVEY GREER QUESTIONED ME REGARDING A RECENT SERIES OF CRIMES IN YOUR CITY'S BACKBONE DISTRICT.

DREAD RESERVATION WAS FORMED AS A STIPULATION OF THE 2039 ACCORD, AND IT'S WIDELY BELIEVED THAT YOU HAVE NEVER TRAVELED BEYOND ITS BORDERS--

--ALLEGING THERE ARE SOME WHO WOULD SEEK TO HAVE YOU KILLED. WHAT CONNECTION COULD YOU HAVE TO CRIMES COMMITTED IN A CITY YOU HAVEN'T ENTERED IN FIFTEEN YEARS?

LIEUTENANT GREER DESCRIBED THE CRIMES AS "ANTI-SURROGATE." HE, LIKE SO MANY OTHERS, THINKS I AM ALONE IN MY BELIEF THAT THESE ABOMINATIONS ARE BLASPHEMY.
THEREFORE, I MUST BE RESPONSIBLE.

FOR THE BENEFIT OF THOSE VIEWERS WHO MAY NOT BE FAMILIAR, PLEASE EXPLAIN YOUR POSITION REGARDING THE SURROGATE QUESTION.

STREICHER lager
SURROGATES ARE A VAIN ATTEMPT TO IMPROVE UPON GOD'S ALREADY PERFECT WILL.
THEY REPRESENT THE WORST EFFORTS OF MEN TO SUPERCEDE GOD AND BECOME GODS THEMSELVES.

AS WITH THE TOWER OF BABEL, ALL WHO SEEK TO RAISE EARTH TO HEAVEN WILL MEET WITH GOD'S WRATH.

IS THAT HOW YOU SEE THESE CRIMES, AS EXAMPLES OF DIVINE PUNISHMENT?

NOAH'S FLOOD. SODOM AND GOMORRAH.
TIME AND AGAIN GOD HAS SHOWN THAT HIS JUDGMENT ON THOSE WHO RENOUNCE HIM IS SWIFT AND ABSOLUTE.

WHAT MESSAGE DO YOU HAVE FOR THE PEOPLE OF CENTRAL GEORGIA METROPOLIS?

A SHEPHERD SERVES BEST WHEN TENDING TO HIS FLOCK, BUT THE LORD ALSO ASKED THAT HIS DISCIPLES BE FISHERS OF MEN.

I ASKED YOU HERE SO I MIGHT TELL THE CITY THAT, EVEN THOUGH THE LORD'S JUDGMENT IS UPON US, IT IS NEVER TOO LATE TO CHOOSE THE PATH OF RIGHTEOUSNESS.
ONLY THROUGH REPENTANCE CAN GOD'S MERCY BE RECEIVED.

THANK YOU, MR. POWELL, AND THANK YOU FOR INVITING US HERE TODAY.

NOW BACK TO YOU, DOUG.
THANK YOU, DONNA.
HERE TO GIVE US SOME INSIGHT ON THIS INTERVIEW IS GNN ANALYST--
SO MUCH FOR NOT SITTING DOWN WITH ABOMINATIONS.

YOU HAVE A CALL.

GREER.

I UNDERSTAND YOU MUST BE VERY BUSY, BUT I WAS HOPING YOU MIGHT HAVE TIME TO EXPLAIN WHAT I JUST WATCHED.

I'M SORRY I HAVEN'T FILLED YOU IN, COMMISSIONER, BUT THERE ISN'T THAT MUCH TO REPORT.

TELL THAT TO DONNA REID, LIEUTENANT.
NOW WHERE ARE YOU ON THIS THING?

RIGHT NOW WE'RE NOWHERE.
TWO SURRIES WERE DELIBERATELY FRIED IN A BACKBONE ALLEY ON MAY 8. THE FOLLOWING NIGHT A SIMILAR CRIME TOOK PLACE AT CLARK TECHNOLOGIES, WHERE THE PERP MADE OFF WITH A HIGH-TECH COMPUTER CHIP.

I'M WAITING FOR YOU TO EXPLAIN WHY YOU WENT TO THE PROPHET.
commissioner grillo

THIS COMPUTER CHIP, IT'S REAL NEXT-GENERATION STUFF. IT USES ELECTROMAGNETIC PULSES TO DISRUPT ELECTRONIC SYSTEMS.
WE THINK OUR GUY'S PLANNING TO WIPE OUT THE CITY'S SURROGATE POPULATION.

THE GOOD NEWS IS THE CHIP WON'T WORK WITHOUT THE SOFTWARE, WHICH IS SAFE AND SOUND AT CDV LABS. THE BUILDING'S UNDER ROUND-THE-CLOCK SURVEILLANCE, SO WE'LL BE READY IF HE SHOWS.

GOD HELP US IF THE PRESS GETS WIND OF ***THIS***. YOU THINK THE PROPHET'S PULLING THE STRINGS?

HE'S GOT THE RESOURCES AND PLENTY OF VOLUNTEERS, AND I DON'T HAVE TO TELL YOU HOW MUCH HE HATES SURRIES.

STILL, TALKING TO HIM WAS A MISTAKE. THE PRESS IS GOING TO BE ALL OVER YOU NOW.
"***NO***" AND "***COMMENT***" ARE THE ONLY TWO WORDS IN YOUR VOCABULARY. UNDERSTOOD?

I'M LEAVING YOU ON THE CASE BECAUSE, FRANKLY, YOU'RE THE BEST I'VE GOT. BUT I'LL BE EXPECTING FREQUENT PROGRESS REPORTS, HARVEY.
MAKE ME PROUD.

YES, SIR. THANK YOU, COMMISSIONER.

HE SAW THE NEWSCAST.
HARV, *EVERYBODY* SAW THE NEWSCAST.

THE PROPHET JUST MADE MY LIFE-- AND THIS CASE-- A WHOLE LOT HARDER.

I THOUGHT SHOWING UP ON HIS DOORSTEP WOULD CATCH HIM OFF GUARD, BUT I PLAYED RIGHT INTO HIS HANDS.

WE DON'T HAVE THE MANPOWER TO DEAL WITH THE CITYWIDE PANIC THAT BROADCAST WILL START--
--NEVERMIND THE PRESS FOLLOWING US LIKE PAPARAZZI AND BROADCASTING TO THE TELEVISED WORLD OUR EVERY MOVE.

SPEAKING OF WHICH . . . DID YOU TELL THE COMMISSIONER YOU WERE WORKING THIS CASE LIVE?
HE'S GOT ENOUGH TO RIP ME ABOUT. I FIGURE I'LL SAVE THAT FOR WHEN HE'S IN A BETTER MOOD. WHY?

OH, NOTHING. BUT YOU MIGHT WANT TO STASH THAT CUT HAND IN YOUR POCKET.

LIEUTENANT GREER, IS IT TRUE THAT
DO YOU HAVE ANY EVIDENCE LINKING ZAIRE POWELL
ANY INFORMATION ABOUT THE CRIMES COMMITTED?
SEARCHING FOR A SUSPECT?
SHOULD THE PEOPLE OF CENTRAL GEORGIA METROPOLIS BE WORRIED?

THERE'S NO REASON FOR THE PEOPLE OF CENTRAL GEORGIA METROPOLIS TO NOT GO ABOUT THEIR LIVES AS USUAL.

BEYOND THAT, I'M AFRAID I CAN'T COMMENT ON AN ONGOING INVESTIGATION.

HOW CAN YOU BE SURE THE CITIZENS ARE NOT
WHAT WILL BE THE DEPARMENT'S COURSE OF ACTION IF
WHAT DOES THIS MEAN FOR THE 2039 ACCORD?

ADMITTING THE PRESS MAY NOT HAVE BEEN WISE, YOUR EMINENCE.
WHAT IS YOUR CONCERN, MINISTER? I HAVE DONE NOTHING FOR WHICH I SHOULD HIDE.

PERHAPS NOT, BUT ONE MUST AVOID THE *APPEARANCE* OF IMPROPRIETY.

IF THE POLICE SHOULD DISCOVER, OR MANUFACTURE, ANY EVIDENCE CONNECTING YOU TO THESE CRIMES, THEY WON'T HESITATE TO--
I ASSURE YOU THAT WILL NOT HAPPEN.

YOU CONFUSE ME, MINISTER. THIS IS A TIME OF GREAT REJOICING. WE HAVE PRAYED FOR THE DAY OF DELIVERANCE, AND AT LAST IT IS UPON US--

--YET YOU HAVE NOT THE FAITH TO ACCEPT THAT THE LORD WILL SEE IT THROUGH TO ITS END. I EXPECT MORE FROM MY SECOND.

FORGIVE ME, YOUR EMINENCE, BUT MY FAITH IS NOT THE ISSUE. THE LORD'S JUDGMENT WILL SURELY BE AS SWIFT AND FINAL AS YOU HAVE FORSEEN.

I AM MERELY SUGGESTING THAT WE PREPARE OURSELVES. DID NOT THE JEWS WASH THEIR DOORS WITH LAMB'S BLOOD TO WARD AGAINST--

I DO NOT NEED A LESSON IN THE SCRIPTURES FROM *YOU*, XAVIER. YOU FORGET YOURSELF.

AGAIN, I BEG YOUR FORGIVENESS, YOUR EMINENCE. I ONLY WISH TO SAY THAT I FIND NO HARM IN TAKING CAUTION.

VERY WELL. WHAT DO YOU RECOMMEND?

THE RESERVATION'S STOCKPILES ARE DANGEROUSLY LOW. IF WE BEGIN CONSERVING FOOD AND WATER IMMEDIATELY, WE WILL BE BETTER PREPARED FOR A SIEGE.

AND ALL MALES ABOVE SIXTEEN SHOULD REPORT TO THEIR LOCAL STEWARDS FOR INSTRUCTION.
THEY NEED TO BE REMINDED WHAT IS EXPECTED OF THEM SHOULD WE BE ATTACKED.

WE MUST BE READY FOR EVERY EVENTUALITY.
I WILL ADDRESS YOUR CONCERNS DURING TONIGHT'S SERMON. WILL THAT BE SATISFACTORY?

YOUR WISDOM PREVAILS.
YOUR EMINENCE?

WHAT IS IT, ACOLYTE?
THE PEOPLE HAVE GATHERED FOR THE EVENING SERMON.

IN THE NAME OF THE FATHER, THE SON--

--AND THE HOLY SPIRIT.

LET US PRAY . . .

OKAY, EVERYBODY. I KNOW THIS IS OUR THIRD NIGHT, IT'S *WAY* PAST OUR BEDTIME, AND WE'D ALL RATHER BE DOING SOMETHING ELSE, BUT LET'S STAY SHARP. GIVE ME A ROLL CALL.
ALPHA TEAM, CHECK.
BRAVO TEAM, CHECK.

CHARLIE TEAM, CHECK.
DELTA TEAM, CHECK.
ECHO TEAM, CHECK.

NICE WEATHER, DON'T YOU THINK, HARV? YOU WISHING YOU TOOK THAT REPLACEMENT YET?

ARE YOU KIDDING? I HAVEN'T FELT THIS IN *YEARS*.

I THOUGHT IT'D BE MISERABLE, BUT THERE'S SOMETHING *REJUVENATING* ABOUT IT.
IT REMINDS ME OF RUNNING THROUGH THE SPRINKLERS WHEN I WAS A KID.

GOOD FOR YOU. I CAN'T WAIT TO HEAR WHAT PNEUMONIA REMINDS YOU OF.
VERY FUNNY.
HEY, PARTNER. YOU GET THE FEELING WE'RE NOT THE ONLY ONES KEEPING WATCH UP HERE?
SWAT
SWAT

YOU MEAN LIKE LUMBERJACK'S BEEN--
*STEEPLE*JACK, FOR CHRIST'S SAKE.

--WHATEVER. LIKE HE'S BEEN STAKING *US* OUT? YEAH, I'VE THOUGHT ABOUT IT. WISH I KNEW WHAT HE WAS WAITING FOR.

LIEUTENANT, THIS IS BRAVO TEAM LEADER. DO WE HAVE A BIRD UP TONIGHT?
NEGATIVE, BRAVO. WE HAVE NO BIRD IN THE AIR.

WELL, WE CAN HEAR ONE COMING.

HOW THE HELL DID *THEY* FIND US?

GNN

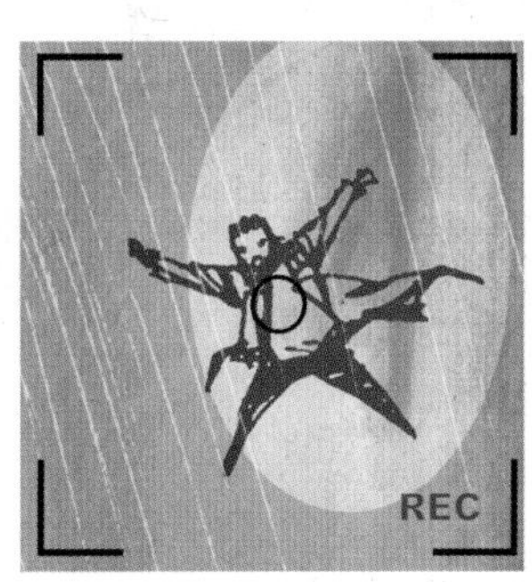
REC

CHARLIE TEAM LEADER, THIS IS DELTA. DO YOU SEE SOMETHING MOVING ON BUILDING FIVE?
NEGATIVE, DELTA.
WAIT. THAT'S AFFIRMATIVE.

ALPHA TEAM LEADER, THIS IS CHARLIE. WE HAVE AN UNKNOWN MOVING ON--
HE *JUMPED!* THE CRAZY BASTARD JUMPED!

METRO POWER

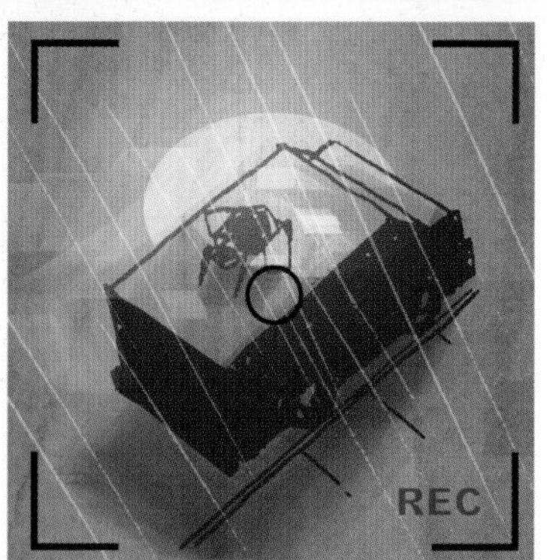
REC

THIS IS LIEUTENANT GREER TO ALL TEAMS. TAKE HIM *DOWN!*

GET THE NEWS-DESK ON THE PHONE.

TELL THEM WE NEED TO GO LIVE. *NOW*.
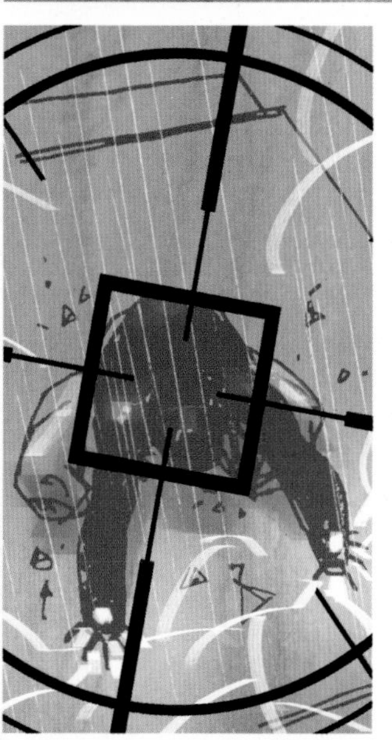

HIT.
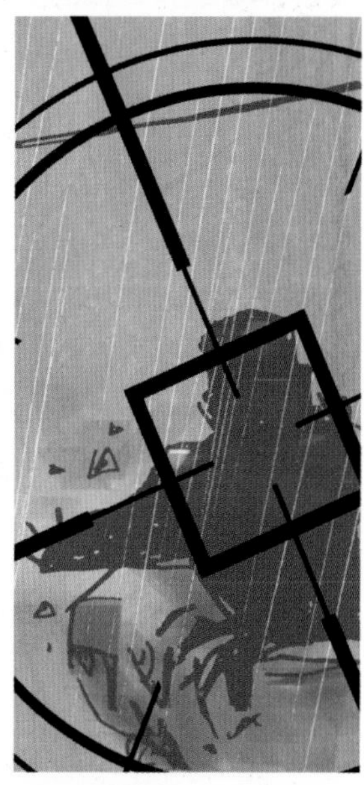

HIT.

EVERYONE HOLD YOUR FIRE. LET THE SCREAMERS DO THEIR JOB.

I DON'T BELIEVE IT . . .

ECHO TEAM IS DOWN. SCREAMERS ARE NOT STOPPING HIM.
SNIPERS, MAINTAIN SURVEILLANCE FROM YOUR POSITIONS. SERGEANT FORD WILL COORDINATE YOUR EFFORTS.

REC
CHARLIE AND DELTA TEAMS ASSAULT THE ROOF--

--ALL OTHER TEAMS ARE ON THE GROUND WITH ME.

ARE YOU GETTING THIS?
I'M ALL OVER IT.

PREPARING TO BLOW THE HATCH.
7 6 5 4 3 2 1

CLEAR!

WE'RE CLEAR UP TOP.
PROCEED AS ORDERED, AND MAINTAIN A SAFE DISTANCE FROM THE PERP AT ALL TIMES.

THOSE REPORTERS DO **NOT** GET PAST YOU, UNDERSTAND?
YES, SIR.

3

CLEAR!
CLEAR!

ASSAULT TEAMS BE ADVISED. THE LAB HAS BEEN BREACHED. THE PERP MAY BE HEADED YOUR WAY. COPY?

ASSAULT TEAMS, DO YOU COPY?

ELVIS IS LEAVING THE BUILDING.

SAY AGAIN. THE PERP HAS EXITED THE BUILDING AND IS ON THE ROOF.

THE PERP IS ON THE ROOF. EVERYBODY OUTSIDE *NOW*.

CAN YOU CUT THAT LINE IN THIS WEATHER?
PIECE OF CAKE, SERGEANT.

GOOD SHOT, SUAREZ.
YEAH, EXCEPT YOU DROPPED HIM RIGHT INTO THE ROTORS.
THIS IS GOING TO BE MESSY . . .

BRAVO, DO YOU HAVE A SHOT?

NEGATIVE. SAY AGAIN, I HAVE NO SHOT.
THERE HE GOES.

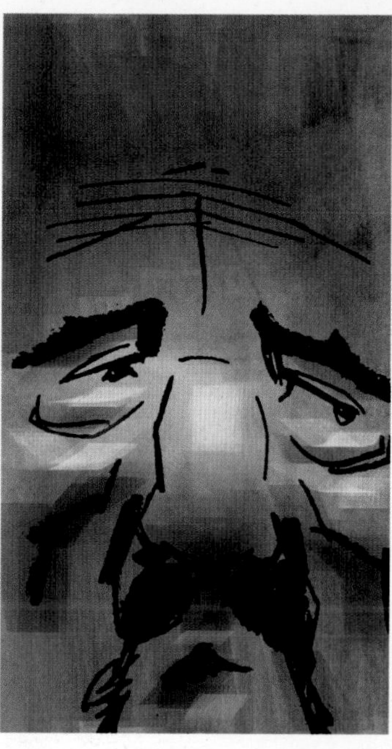

GNN

--ONCE AGAIN, WE ARE BRINGING YOU THIS NEWS AS IT HAPPENS AND WITHOUT THE BENEFIT OF INFORMED COMMENTARY. TRUTHFULLY, WE HAVE NO IDEA WHAT TO MAKE OF WHAT WE'RE SEEING.

WITH US NOW IS LIEUTENANT HARVEY GREER, LEAD INVESTIGATOR AT THE SCENE.
LIEUTENANT GREER, WHAT IS YOUR REACTION TO THE REMARKABLE EVENTS WE JUST WITNESSED?

NO COMMENT.

dail@ tablet

AMERICA'S MOST DOWNLOADED PAPER SINCE 2018

VOL. XXXIII · GA EDITION · AUGUST 28, 2039 · $1.00 US

Today's Forecast

H 99.375°F
L 76.625°F

NCAA Outlook

Guru picks the Best and Worst

C-4

AN END TO THE STRIFE

Resolution is reached; city restructuring to begin

ABOVE: Seen together in public for the first time, Mayor Langston and Zaire Powell III, leader of the Dread movement, clasp hands on the steps of City Hall.

BY PAIGE **Costas**

ERIC **Stanley**

Following two days of negotiations, city and state officials together with leaders of the Dread movement reached a resolution yesterday, bringing an end to the riots that have ravaged Central Georgia Metropolis for four days.

The resolution, titled the Joint Cessation Accord, called for concessions on both sides in order to halt the violence that has caused an estimated $200 million in property damage and left 63 dead. Included among the number killed are 27 law enforcement and emergency services personnel.

In a public address announcing the resolution, Mayor Langston (search) said, "This has been a particularly dark and troubling time for our city. But with this accord, we have planted the seed for what we are confident will be a better future for all citizens."

Zaire Powell III (search), the controversial leader of the Dread movement known to his followers as The Prophet, echoed the Mayor's statements. "We have been blessed with great change."

Dawn breaks over "long, uninterrupted night."

For the past four days, daily life in Central Georgia Metropolis ground to a halt as many remained indoors to avoid damage to their surrogate units or, worse, personal attack. Following the news that the riots had ended, however, businesses reopened, and the skywalks were once again teeming with morning commuters.

"It's like the first morning after a long, uninterrupted night," one citizen said.

The riots began on the eve of August 23 in response to a plea bargain accepted earlier that day by three area teens charged with the July beating death of a homeless man. In exchange for pleading guilty to manslaughter, the Office of the District Attorney agreed to sentence the teens as youthful offenders.

Witnesses described the crime saying the teens cornered Zachary Hayes, 52, in an alley and beat him unconscious, despite Hayes defending himself with a length of heavy pipe.

MORE →

"If they were real kids," one witness commented on Hayes's efforts, "they would've run off. But they were surrogates, and they kept coming no matter how many times [Hayes] hit them." Hayes died at Mercy Hospital later that evening.

Tensions over the steadily increasing presence of surrogates had been building for several months as the city's Dread population, consisting primarily of the poor, non-surrogate operating public, felt further marginalized. Hayes's death became a rallying cry for those calling for legal and social reform, many of whom sought to have the teens tried as adults. District Attorney Nicholas Oulette (search) explained his decision to keep the teens in the youthful offender system. "We didn't feel the case was strong enough to guarantee an adult conviction. We compromised in an effort to ensure that some level of justice was reached."

Within hours of the press conference announcing the plea bargain, thousands of Dreads began destroying surrogates, looting storefronts, and setting fire to area buildings. Fourteen citizens died in the blazes, and many more, mistaken on the streets for surrogates, were injured or killed.

Dreads granted reservation status

At the core of the Joint Cessation Accord is the compromise between government officials and Dread leaders that stipulates the withdrawal of all Dreads from the city in exchange for their being granted seventy square miles of undeveloped land southeast of the city. Once the withdrawal is completed, the Dreads will take up permanent residence on the parcel of land and be granted reservation status.

The status permits the Dreads to police and govern themselves, while remaining under the umbrella of state and federal law. No formal announcement has been made, but experts presume that Zaire Powell will head the new Dread government. Powell's anti-surrogate stance on the basis of religious convictions is the foundation of the Dread movement.

Incorporated into the resolution is a four-year, $15 billion aid package designed to provide basic infrastructure, agricultural technology, and food and medical assistance to the new government. Already receiving criticisms for what opponents of the resolution consider to be extreme concessions by the city, Mayor Langston was quick to defend his position. "Mr. Powell and his followers remain citizens of this nation and this state. I think all Georgians understand their obligation to provide assistance where needed."

In a short statement issued by his office, Governor Sandoval (search) signed off on the accord: "Mayor Langston has taken the initiative to stem the violence in his city by drafting a resolution that is beneficial to both parties. As such, he has my approval and my support."

The withdrawal of the Dreads from Metro city limits has already begun and is expected to take no more than five days. Plans are being made to deliver the first wave of assistance by September 3.

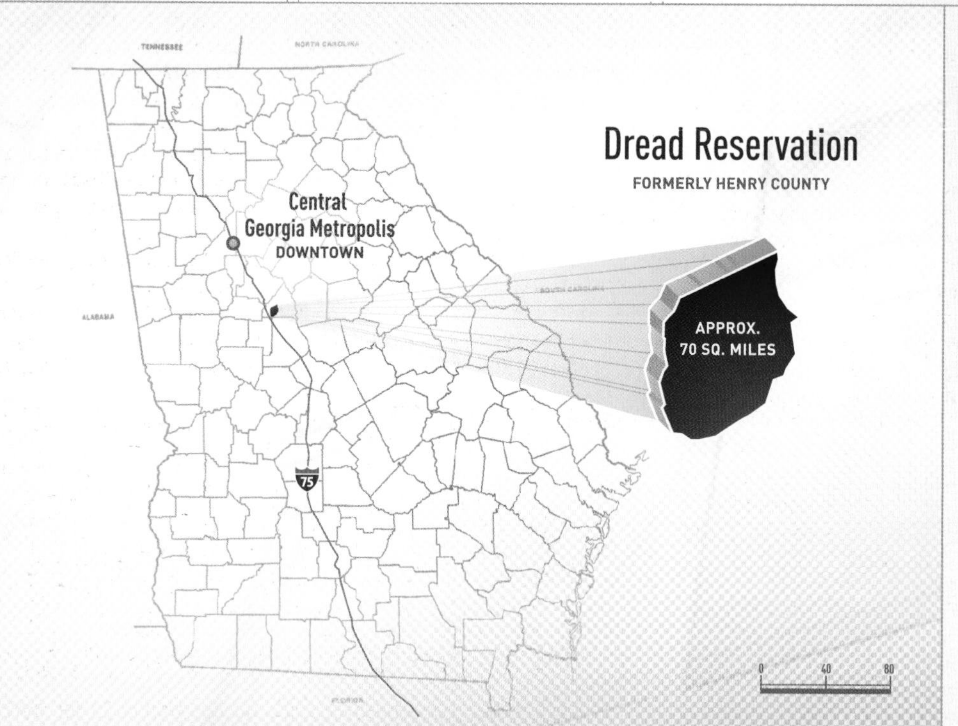

ABOVE: Dread Reservation will be the new home for more than 100,000 Dread citizens.

Officials to Discuss All-Surrogate Police Force

Committee for a Safer Tomorrow head Martino is "open to all suggestions"

BY ALEXIS **Yurgovich**

In an unprecedented development, law enforcement officials in Central Georgia Metropolis will begin hearing proposals next week for moving away from live-body officers and toward an all-surrogate police force. If accepted, the referendum will mark the first time a government entity has endorsed the widespread use of cybernetic substitutes in place of live personnel.

Paul Martino (search), head of the Committee for a Safer Tomorrow, the group charged with modernizing the city's emergency services, backed the discussions.

"It's no secret," Martino said, "that if we'd put surrogate officers into the field sooner, we would've prevented many law enforcement casualties, as well as brought the riots to an earlier conclusion. It would be shortsighted if we did not at least consider utilizing surrogates on a more permanent basis."

When asked about the possibility of expanding the use of surrogates to other emergency services branches, Martino said he is "open to all suggestions" and that he "would not rule out any proposals" at this time.

The proposals being offered vary in scope, with some calling for the immediate replacement of live officers, while others suggest that officers be given the option to operate surrogates at work on a voluntary basis.

With the talks several days away, several organizations are already voicing strong opposition. The website for the public safety group StreetWatch cites concern over the reliability of surrogates, and insists the machines are qualified only for consumer-based recreational use. Leaders of the police and fire department unions have vowed to combat all efforts supporting the use of surrogates, stating that any measure, even those calling for the use of substitutes on a limited or voluntary basis, would be in violation of labor statutes.

Among officers, opinions remain mixed. A recent poll showed only 13% of metro police officers felt the substitution of live officers with surrogates was a good idea, with 38% remaining undecided. 58%, however, saw the additional job safety afforded by operating surrogates in the field as a benefit.

In response to questions regarding the city's ability to pay for a government-mandated surrogate police force, Martino said, "We are only considering the proposals, and any budgetary concerns will be dealt with if and when we enter that phase."

Vigil to be Held for Firefighters Lost in Blaze

BY RONALD **Mills**

A vigil will be held today honoring nine firefighters killed in a fire at the Leftwich Chemicals processing plant on August 26.

The vigil is scheduled to begin at 1:00 p.m. and will take place at the Church of Saint Frances de Sales in the Backbone District. Chief Douglas Kozelak (search) of the metro fire department and Senator Mark Samuelson (search) are expected to attend.

On August 26, emergency services responded to a 911 call alerting them that vandals had set fire to the Leftwich Chemicals plant. The nine firefighters, all from the Backbone District's Ladder Company 12, were searching the interior for occupants when the factory's roof fell in, trapping them in the toxic inferno.

Though the fire, like dozens of others, resulted from the recent wave of anti-surrogate rioting, there are no specific suspects at this time. Arson investigators continue to pursue leads and insist that their inquiry is still in the early stages.

Leftwich Chemicals is the third largest industrial chemical producer in the United States, but it is their relationship with Virtual Self, Inc. (search) that investigators believe led them to become a target for rioters. The chemical giant provides VSI with the base chemicals used in the synthesizing of surrogate skin, hair, and other cosmetics.

The vigil is the first of many ceremonies that will honor emergency services personnel lost in the line of duty during the riots. For more information on this and other ceremonies, citizens should contact the Metro Office of Public Affairs.

ABOVE: The remains of the Leftwich Chemicals processing plant. 9 firefighters were killed when the factory's roof fell in, trapping them in the toxic inferno.

CLASSIFIEDS

SURROGATE SALES & SERVICES

Looking to purchase a pre-owned female surrogate unit for college-bound child. Willing to consider older models, but reliability and proof of upkeep are a must. Youth and physical attractiveness preferred. Call 770-2848-0126 to arrange inspection.

HELP!

Landscaper needs temporary surrogate while primary unit undergoes repairs. Daytime availability and proof of insurance required. Will pay $200/week plus cost of maintenance and cleaning, if necessary. If interested, call 404-4229-8055 ASAP.

Retiring bodyguard with used SU-9 to sell. Traits include: Male, African-American, and imposing height and build. Ideal model for private security work. Cash offers only please. Call 678-9661-5423 and ask for Joe.

SurroMart

NEW AND USED!

Over 100 new and refurbished surrogate units in stock.

▪

Wide selection of models and appearances.

▪

We offer trade and affordable financing. Our staff of consultants is waiting to meet your needs.

SurroMart

Open 9-9 >>Mon-Sat

404-8745-9016

Freelance surrogate technician available. Certified in chassis redesign, cosmetic alteration, and CPU upgrades. Rates vary according to size of job and parts required. References available upon request. Tired of the same old unit? Then call 678-3291-0777.

Donations Needed

Did you know there are thousands of elderly and handicapped people in the metro area who can't afford a surrogate? The Atlanta chapter of the Life-Aid Club is accepting donations of new and used units to help meet this growing need. For directions to a drop-off point near you...

click here

VIRTUAL PERSONALS

SINGLES WANTED

The Fulton County Matchmakers invite all singles eighteen and older to a night of fun and socializing August 30th from 8-11 p.m. at Hogan's Tavern. No matter your age or interests, the Matchmakers will find your mate! $10 cover charge includes complementary appetizers.

Click here for directions

FEELING CURIOUS?

ENJOY EXPERIMENTING?

Attend Swap Meet, the metro area's largest gathering of alternate-lifestyle surrogate operators. Join us the second Tuesday of every month at the Tiffany Club in downtown Old-Atlanta. Both new and experienced users welcome. Must provide proof of age. Click below for details.

www.tiffanyswapmeet.com

SWM seeking SF for adventure and excitement. Enjoys hiking, camping, and extreme sports. I like to travel, and often take trips on a whim. Female operators only please.

Interested? click here

SBF seeking companionship. I'm recently divorced and not looking for anything serious. The past five years were all dinner and a movie, so if you're one to go clubbing until 3 a.m....

click here

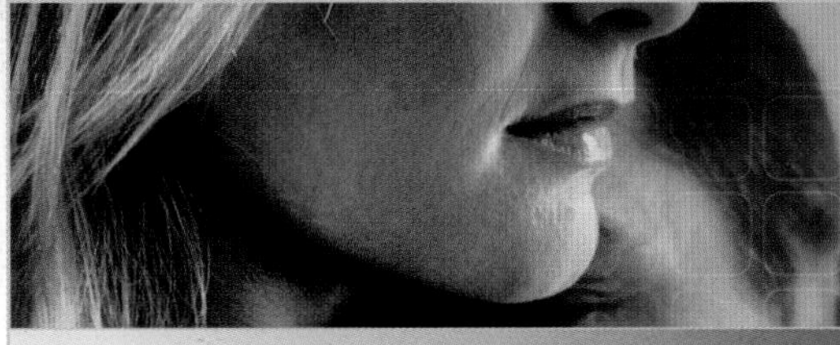
LIFE...ONLY BETTER.
Click here

NEED A DATE ?

EXPERIENCED female companion with many units to choose from. Perfect for casual evenings or formal events. Available 7 days a week. Rates vary. Local engagements only, please. Why go alone?

click here

CLASSIFIED ADS FOR SALE

Reach millions of subscribers in your targeted area daily.

dail@ tablet

EMPLOYMENT FOR OPERATORS

Metro-area sales firm seeks motivated, surrogate-owning individuals to take part in new door-to-door campaign. Our virtual sales technique is a unique approach that combines the personal touch of traditional sales with the ease and comfort of telemarketing. Earn up to $100K/year. To learn more, call us at 404-2776-4521.

Skyline Shine is expanding its downtown office. We need six surrogate owners to form new high-rise cleaning teams. See the city as you never have before! Be willing to work weekends. No experience necessary. $11/hour + unit insurance.

Live Home Work Abroad

Enjoy exotic locales without the worries of travel. America's largest education exchange program needs dedicated, energetic college grads to teach English in foreign countries. Must have B.A. No surrogate? No problem. We have units standing by in classrooms all over the world. Countries will be assigned on a first-come, first-serve basis, so don't delay! For more information, as well as a list of participating countries...

click here

Operators Wanted

S&G Homebuilders has several openings on its all-surrogate crews. We work Mon-Fri, rain or shine. At least 2 years construction experience required. $15/hour + benefits. If interested, download an application below....

click here

United Guaranty is hiring experienced drivers for its armored car division. Clean driving record and minimum Class B Driver License required. All applicants must be able to provide their own surrogate. Starting salary is $500/week. Call 678-7963-0001 for details.

dail@ tablet

AMERICA'S MOST DOWNLOADED PAPER SINCE 2018

chapter
FOUR

Biologics

ONCE AGAIN, YOU ARE WATCHING FOOTAGE FROM A 3:00 A.M. BREAK-IN AT CDV LABS, WHERE A ***LONE*** ASSAILANT PROVED TOO MUCH FOR AT LEAST ***FIFTEEN*** METRO POLICE OFFICERS AND S.W.A.T. PERSONNEL.
GNN-TV

THE ONLY EVIDENCE LEFT AT THE SCENE-- THE ***ARM*** OF THE ASSAILANT'S SURROGATE, SEVERED DURING A COLLISION WITH OUR OWN GNN NEWS HELICOPTER.
GNN-TV

THE SENIOR OFFICER ON THE SCENE, LIEUTENANT HARVEY GREER, DECLINED TO COMMENT, BUT A POLICE SPOKESPERSON IS DESCRIBING THE BREAK-IN AS AN ACT OF INDUSTRIAL ESPIONAGE.
GNN-TV

SOME, HOWEVER, SEE LIEUTENANT GREER'S PRESENCE AS A LINK TO A RECENT STRING OF UNSOLVED ***ANTI-SURROGATE*** CRIMES, AND THEY ARE CALLING THIS THE WORK OF A ***TECHNO-TERRORIST***.
GNN-TV

WITH US IN THE STUDIO TO HELP SORT THROUGH THIS ARE RETIRED METRO POLICE CAPTAIN DAVID PATTON, AND ANDREW GREENE, AN INDUSTRIAL SECURITY EXPERT WITH MCNAB CONSULTING.
I'LL PUT THE QUESTION TO YOU FIRST, DAVID: TECHNO-TERRORISM OR INDUSTRIAL ESPIONAGE?

EVERYONE ***LOVES*** A COVER-UP, BOB, BUT UNTIL THE POLICE RELEASE MORE INFORMATION, THERE IS NO NEED TO SEE THIS AS AN ACT OF TERRORISM.
BUT THEY'RE ***NOT*** RELEASING INFORMATION. LOOK, BOB, IF THIS GUY IS JUST A BURGLAR, THEN WHY HAVEN'T WE BEEN TOLD WHAT WAS STOLEN? THERE'S MORE TO LAST NIGHT'S EVENTS THAN POLICE ARE LETTING ON . . .

YOU'RE ALL OVER THE MORNING NEWS.
NOT NOW, MARGARET. I JUST STOPPED IN FOR A CHANGE OF CLOTHES.

WHAT IS IT, HARVEY? WHAT DOES HE WANT?
WHAT ELSE? TO CHANGE THE WORLD.

HE WANTS TO DESTROY ALL OF THE CITY'S SURROGATES--
--AND AFTER LAST NIGHT, HE HAS THE MEANS TO DO IT.

WHY WOULD ANYONE DO SUCH A THING?

WHY? BECAUSE HE SEES WHERE THE WORLD IS HEADED. CITIES FILLED WITH PEOPLE WHO AREN'T REALLY PEOPLE. LIFE REDUCED TO A DATA FEED.

YOU SOUND LIKE YOU'RE ON HIS SIDE.

MY JOB PREVENTS ME FROM BEING ON HIS SIDE, BUT I DO UNDERSTAND HIM.
I'VE SEEN THE EFFECT SURROGATES CAN HAVE ON PEOPLE. I SEE IT EVERY DAY.

PEOPLE? WHY DON'T YOU JUST SAY IT, HARVEY? YOU MEAN ME.

THIS ISN'T YOU. DEEP DOWN YOU KNOW IT, BUT YOU WON'T ACCEPT IT. AND IT'S DESTROYING OUR MARRIAGE.

AREN'T YOU SO HOLIER-THAN-THOU. YOU DON'T LINK FOR A FEW DAYS, AND THAT MAKES YOU SOME KIND OF A ROLE MODEL?
I'M NOT THE PROBLEM IN THIS MARRIAGE. IT'S YOU AND YOUR CONDESCENSION.

PUT IT AWAY, MARGARET. JUST FOR A FEW DAYS. AREN'T YOU AT LEAST WILLING TO TRY?
I HAVE A RIGHT TO LIVE MY LIFE HOWEVER I CHOOSE. WITH OR WITHOUT YOUR APPROVAL!

IS THAT WHAT YOU THINK, THAT I'M JUDGING YOU? IS IT SO HARD TO BELIEVE THAT I LOVE YOU?
SPARE ME.
YOU HAVE A CALL.

GREER.
OKAY, PETE. TELL SCREWS I'LL BE THERE IN TWENTY MINUTES.

I'VE GOT TO GO.

THAT'S RIGHT. DO YOUR JOB, LIEUTENANT.
GO PROTECT THE LIFESTYLES OF ME AND EVERYONE ELSE YOU PITY!

MAY 13, 2054.

REMARKABLE . . .

SIMPLY ***REMARKABLE***.

OKAY, SCREWS, WE'RE ALL HERE. CAN WE GET ON WITH IT?
CERTAINLY. LET'S BEGIN WITH THE CLOTHING.
WHAT WE'RE LOOKING AT HERE IS PART OF AN INSULATING BODYSUIT ENGINEERED TO ABSORB, STORE, AND RECHANNEL ELECTRICAL ENERGY.

YOU SEE THESE SMALL, METAL DISKS?
RECHARGEABLE BATTERIES. JUDGING BY THE NUMBER HERE, I'D GUESS THE ENTIRE GARMENT CONTAINS SOMEWHERE IN THE NEIGHBORHOOD OF TWO HUNDRED CELLS--

--HAVING A COMBINED STORAGE CAPACITY IN EXCESS OF ONE ***BILLION*** VOLTS.
THAT'S THE EQUIVALENT OF A LIGHTNING BOLT.

SO THIS GUY SITS HOME ALL DAY WITH A CORD UP HIS ASS, THEN GOES OUT AT NIGHT AND SHOCKS PEOPLE?
I'D HATE TO HAVE HIS POWER BILL.

NOT EXACTLY. THESE BATTERIES NOT ONLY STORE ELECTRICITY, THEY ALSO ***COLLECT*** IT.
THEY SAP ELECTROSTATIC ENERGY OUT OF THE SURROUNDING ENVIRONMENT AND STORE THE CUMULATIVE CHARGE.

THAT'S WHY HE COMES AND GOES WITH THE STORMS--THE SUIT OPERATES ON THE STATIC FIELDS INHERENT IN THOSE WEATHER CONDITIONS.
IN EFFECT, IT HARNESSES THE FLASH STORMS' POWER.

LIGHTNING IN A BOTTLE.
YOU GOT IT. AND WHAT'S EVEN MORE INTERESTING IS HOW HE APPLIES THE ENERGY ONCE HE'S GATHERED IT.

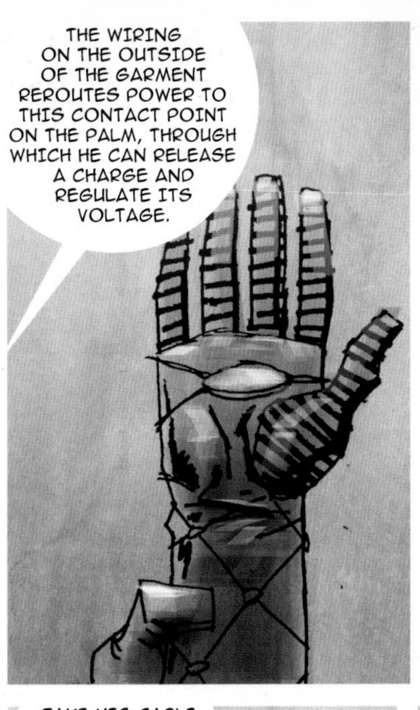
THE WIRING ON THE OUTSIDE OF THE GARMENT REROUTES POWER TO THIS CONTACT POINT ON THE PALM, THROUGH WHICH HE CAN RELEASE A CHARGE AND REGULATE ITS VOLTAGE.

WE'VE ALL SEEN WHAT HAPPENS WHEN HE GOES FULL-BORE--SURROGATES DAMAGED BEYOND REPAIR, ENTIRE INDUSTRIAL COMPLEXES THROWN INTO BLACKOUT.
BUT HE CAN ALSO USE ELECTRICITY IN MUCH SUBTLER WAYS.

TAKE HIS CABLE GUN, FOR EXAMPLE. THIS THIN FILAMENT IS WOVEN FROM AN EXTREMELY STRONG, YET PLIABLE METAL ALLOY--
--WHICH IS ENCASED IN A COMPLEX SLEEVE MODELED AFTER HUMAN MUSCULATURE.

WATCH WHAT HAPPENS WHEN A SMALL CHARGE IS SENT THROUGH THE CABLE.

SEE HOW THE END WRAPS AROUND THE PENCIL? IT'LL STAY LIKE THAT UNTIL THE FLOW OF ELECTRICITY IS STOPPED.

THE CONTRACTION MIMICS A MUSCLE'S RESPONSE TO ELECTRICAL STIMULUS. IT ENABLES HIM TO LATCH ON TO THINGS FOR AS LONG AS THE CHARGE IS MAINTAINED.
BY DIRECTING MORE POWER TO THE GUN'S CRANK MECHANISM, HE CAN REEL HIMSELF IN, AND AWAY HE GOES.

HE EVEN HAS DIFFERENT ATTACHMENTS FOR THE CABLE.

I THOUGHT YOU WERE KIDDING ABOUT THE CLAW, HARV.
DAMN NEAR TOOK MY ARM OFF IN THAT SKYWALK.
THERE'S ALSO A SLOT FOR THIS SIMPLE WEIGHT ATTACHMENT, PROBABLY USED TO HELP THE CABLE SAIL FARTHER. WE FOUND IT AT THE END OF THE SEVERED LINE ON THE ROOFTOP.

THE ENTIRE SYSTEM HAS A LEVEL OF SOPHISTICATION I'VE NOT SEEN BEFORE. I'VE NEVER EVEN *READ* ABOUT SOMETHING LIKE THIS.
IT'S QUITE FASCINATING, REALLY.

WELL, WE ALREADY KNEW THE GUY WAS SMART. SO WHAT CAN YOU TELL ME ABOUT THE SURRIE?
THE CONSTRUCTION'S A BIT DATED, BUT OTHER THAN THAT IT'S GARDEN-VARIETY.
EXCEPT FOR ONE THING--THERE ARE NO UNIT IDENTIFICATION NUMBERS ON ANY OF THE COMPONENT PARTS.

HOW CAN THAT BE? DOESN'T VIRTUAL SELF STAMP ALL OF THEIR PARTS WITH UINS DURING PRODUCTION?
YES, BUT THE FACT REMAINS THAT THIS SURROGATE DOESN'T HAVE ANY.
AND WITHOUT THEM, THERE'S NO WAY TO TRACE IT BACK TO ITS OWNER.

WHAT ABOUT A KNOCKOFF?
MANUFACTURING SURROGATES IS A DIFFICULT PROCESS, SERGEANT. YOU DON'T BAKE THEM IN AN OVEN.

THE COSMETICS ALONE REQUIRE CHEMICALS AND EQUIPMENT FOUND ONLY IN INDUSTRIAL SETTINGS, NEVERMIND THE CIRCUITRY AND CHASSIS CONSTRUCTION.
I DON'T THINK A PIRATE OPERATION IS POSSIBLE, BUT, IF IT IS, VSI WOULD KNOW HOW IT COULD BE DONE.

THEN I GUESS WE NEED TO ASK THEM SOME QUESTIONS.
THEY SHOULD BE IN SOON. WE'LL WAIT A LITTLE BIT AND TRY TO CATCH THEM AT THE OFFICE.

IN THE MEANTIME, SEND THE COMMISSIONER A COPY OF WHAT YOU'VE GOT, SCREWS, AND TELL HIM I'M FOLLOWING UP ON A LEAD.
WILL DO, LIEUTENANT.

VSI
DID IT FREAK YOU OUT, HARV? I MEAN, DID YOU THINK HE WAS A SURROGATE?

I WOULDN'T SAY I EXPECTED IT. IT SEEMS A LITTLE TOO HYPOCRITICAL, EVEN FOR THE PROPHET.
WHAT SURPRISED ME WAS THE WAY HE SHOOK OFF THE SCREAMERS. I HAVE YET TO MEET THE OPERATOR WHO DIDN'T TEAR OFF HIS HEADSET AT THE SOUND OF ***THOSE*** THINGS.

WHAT IF THERE ISN'T AN OPERATOR? YOU KNOW, ARTIFICIAL INTELLIGENCE.

MY GOD, YOU MEAN SOMEHOW THE SURROGATE IS ***ALIVE***, AND IT WANTS PEOPLE TO STOP REJECTING THE VERY HUMANITY IT LONGS FOR? THAT MAKES ***PERFECT*** SENSE!

ARE YOU SERIOUS? A.I.?
THERE'S A BIG DIFFERENCE BETWEEN PLAYING A BANG-UP GAME OF CHESS AND ***ACTUAL THOUGHT***. YOU WATCH TOO MANY SCI-FI MOVIES.

IT'S 9:15. LET'S GO SEE IF THEY'RE IN.

AND KEEP THE SUPER-ROBOT THEORY TO YOURSELF. I'M CATCHING ENOUGH HELL AS IT IS.
YEAH, YEAH.

I'M LIEUTENANT GREER, AND THIS IS SERGEANT FORD. WHO'S THE HIGHEST RANKING COMPANY OFFICIAL CURRENTLY ON THE PREMISES?
VSI
THAT WOULD BE OUR CEO, VICTOR WELCH.

WE'LL NEED TO SPEAK WITH HIM, PLEASE.
JUST A MOMENT.

MR. WELCH? THERE ARE TWO METRO POLICE DETECTIVES HERE TO SEE YOU.
THEY HAVEN'T SAID.
YES. RIGHT AWAY.

MR. WELCH HAS AN ENGAGEMENT DOWNTOWN IN THIRTY MINUTES, BUT YOU MAY MEET WITH HIM UNTIL HIS CAR ARRIVES.

THESE ARE THE GENTLEMEN I WAS TELLING YOU ABOUT, MR. WELCH.
THANK YOU, GINNY.

LIEUTENANT HARVEY GREER AND SERGEANT PETE FORD. THANK YOU FOR TAKING THE TIME.
NOT AT ALL.
VICTOR WELCH. PLEASE, HAVE A SEAT.

SOMETHING'S COME UP IN ONE OF OUR INVESTIGATIONS, AND WE WERE HOPING YOU MIGHT BE ABLE TO SHED SOME LIGHT ON IT.
DOES IT HAVE ANYTHING TO DO WITH WHAT HAPPENED LAST NIGHT AT CDV LABS?

I RECOGNIZE YOU FROM THE NEWS.

I'M SORRY, BUT I CAN'T COMMENT ON AN ONGOING INVESTIGATION.

I UNDERSTAND.
SO, HOW CAN I HELP THE POLICE DEPARTMENT?

IT'S OUR UNDERSTANDING THAT ALL SURROGATES ARE GIVEN REGISTRATION NUMBERS BEFORE LEAVING THE FACTORY. IS THAT CORRECT?

OF COURSE. FROM THE BEGINNING, VSI WAS MINDFUL OF THE POTENTIAL FOR SURROGATE CHOP SHOPS AND A BLACK MARKET CULTURE.

OUR POLICY IS SIMPLE, AND WE DON'T DEVIATE FROM IT. ONCE A CUSTOMER ORDERS A UNIT--AND AFTER THE FINANCING IS APPROVED--IT'S ASSIGNED A UNIT IDENTIFICATION NUMBER.
DURING THE MANUFACTURING PROCESS THE UIN IS ETCHED INTO ALL OF THE COMPONENT PARTS, AND A BARCODE BEARING THE NUMBER IS STAMPED INTO THE COSMETICS AT THE BASE OF THE UNIT'S NECK.

WHAT WOULD HAPPEN IF A SURROGATE SOMEHOW SKIPPED THE REGISTRATION STAGE?
FOR STARTERS, WE WOULDN'T KNOW WHO TO DELIVER IT TO. MORE IMPORTANTLY, THE UNIT WOULD HAVE NO SIGNAL ADDRESS.

YOU SEE, PAIRED WITH EACH UIN IS A UNIQUE SIGNAL ADDRESS, THROUGH WHICH THE REGISTERED UNIT IS ABLE TO COMMUNICATE WITH OUR TRANSMISSION SATELLITES VIA THE MAINFRAMES LOCATED HERE, AT OUR HOME OFFICE.

WITHOUT REGISTRATION, THERE'S NO WAY TO GUARANTEE THAT THE SAME ADDRESS WON'T BE ASSIGNED TWICE. IMAGINE THE ***CHAOS***--LEGAL AND OTHERWISE--THAT WOULD ARISE FROM OVERLAPPING SIGNALS.

OUR PEOPLE TELL US THAT SURROGATES CAN'T BE MANUFACTURED OUTSIDE OF FACTORY SETTINGS. WHAT'S YOUR OPINION ON THAT?

I REALLY COULDN'T SAY. MY EXPERTISE IS BUSINESS, NOT SCIENCE.
THE PERSON WHO WOULD BE OF THE MOST USE TO YOU IN THAT REGARD IS LIONEL CANTER.

AS IN ***LIONEL CANTER***, THE GUY WHO INVENTED THE SURROGATE?

"INVENTED" IS A STRONG WORD, SERGEANT. VSI WAS EXCELLING IN CYBERNETICS AND VIRTUAL REALITY LONG BEFORE LIONEL CANTER CAME ALONG. HE MERELY FOUND A WAY TO MARRY THE TWO TECHNOLOGIES.
ANYWAY, HE DESIGNED OUR EARLIEST PRODUCTION PROTOCOLS.

IS HE IN THE BUILDING?
HE RETIRED TWO YEARS AGO. I BELIEVE HE'S DOING FREELANCE CONSULTING NOW.
HIS ABSENCE IS FELT, ESPECIALLY NOW WHEN WE'RE ABOUT TO ROLL OUT OUR NEW YOUTH INITIATIVE.

YOUTH INITIATIVE? I THOUGHT VSI HAD A POLICY AGAINST UNDERAGE OPERATORS.
THINGS HAVE COME A LONG WAY SINCE THE ZACHARY HAYES BEATING, LIEUTENANT.

SURROGATES ARE THIS COUNTRY'S WAY OF LIFE NOW, AND WE SHOULDN'T LET THE MISTAKE OF THREE TEENS--FIFTEEN YEARS AGO--PREVENT OUR CHILDREN FROM BEING A PART OF IT.
TO THAT END, WE'RE INTRODUCING A LINE OF UNITS DESIGNED SPECIFICALLY FOR THE UNDER-EIGHTEEN MARKET.

IMAGINE PARENTS NOT HAVING TO WORRY ABOUT THEIR CHILDREN GETTING ABDUCTED FROM THE MALL, OR CAUGHT IN THE CROSSFIRE OF A SCHOOL SHOOTING.
IMAGINE ADOLESCENTS NOT HAVING TO COPE WITH THE PAINFUL ISSUES OF BODY IMAGE AND PEER PRESSURE. NO MORE BULLYING. NO MORE TEEN PREGNANCY.

SURROGATES WILL PROVIDE PEACE OF MIND FOR PARENTS, AND A HEALTHIER, HAPPIER ENVIRONMENT FOR CHILDREN.
EVERYBODY WINS.

WE EXPECT PROFITS TO GO THROUGH THE ROOF.
MR. WELCH? YOUR CAR HAS ARRIVED.

THANK YOU, GINNY. TELL THEM I'LL BE RIGHT DOWN. AND HAVE PERSONNEL GET THE DETECTIVES MR. CANTER'S ADDRESS.

CAN I ASK ABOUT YOUR HAND, LIEUTENANT?
MY UNIT'S HAVING SOME WORK DONE.

MIGHT I SUGGEST AN UPGRADE? TAKE ONE OF OUR BROCHURES. THERE ARE SOME EXCITING NEW FEATURES THAT MIGHT INTEREST YOU. IT'S ON US.
THAT'S A GENEROUS OFFER.

IT'S OUR PLEASURE. WE'RE ALWAYS WILLING TO HELP OUT THE BOYS IN BLUE. BESIDES, IT'S GOOD P.R.
CHOOSE YOURSELF

NOW IF YOU'LL EXCUSE ME, I HAVE TO BE DOWNTOWN IN TWENTY MINUTES. GINNY WILL SEE YOU OUT.
WE APPRECIATE THE INFORMATION, MR. WELCH.
ANYTIME. GINNY ALWAYS KNOWS WHERE TO FIND ME.

BLOCK 4290, BUILDING 18. PENTHOUSE SUITE. VERY NICE.
THAT'S NOT FAR FROM HERE. MIGHT AS WELL GO NOW.

WHEN WE CATCH UP WITH FLAPJACK--
STEEPLEJACK.
--DO YOU THINK I CAN GET HIM TO DROP ME FROM A SKYWALK? I COULD USE AN UPGRADE.

CHECK OUT SOME OF THESE NEW FEATURES: TASK MEMORY. SELF-CLEANING ABDOMINAL RESERVOIRS.
YOU CAN EVEN PROGRAM A SEQUENCE OF MOVEMENTS TO MAKE IT LOOK LIKE YOU'RE LINKED WHILE YOU'RE ON THE CAN.

LISTEN TO THIS: "CHOOSE A SET OF CLIMATIC CONDITIONS, AND YOUR SURROGATE MAINTAINS THEM DURING ANY WEATHER. WITH FORECAST MANAGER,™ EVERY DAY IS THE PERFECT DAY."

NO MORE STORMS. WHAT DO YOU THINK, HARV?

I'M NOT GETTING ANOTHER SURRIE.
WHAT? YOU MEAN NOT EVER?

NOT EVER. I'M STAYING AS IS.
YOU'RE SERIOUS. WHY?

I JUST DON'T WANT IT ANYMORE. YOU KNOW, WHEN SURRIES FIRST CAME ON THE SCENE, THEY SOUNDED LIKE A GOOD THING--

--NO MORE WORRYING THAT WHEN YOU LEFT TO WORK YOUR SHIFT, YOU MIGHT NOT COME HOME. WHAT COP WOULDN'T WANT A SAFER JOB AND MORE SECURITY FOR HIS FAMILY?

BUT IT'S NO LONGER A ***SAFETY*** THING AS MUCH AS A ***LIFESTYLE*** THING. ENHANCED LOOKS, DATA PLAYBACK, FORECAST MANAGER!™
AT WHAT POINT DO YOU STOP BEING YOU?

LOSING MY SURRIE WAS THE BEST THING THAT COULD'VE HAPPENED. IT MADE ME REALIZE WHAT I WAS MISSING. FROM NOW ON I'M GOING TO ***LIVE*** MY LIFE. AND WHEN I'M TOO OLD TO CUT IT, I'LL RETIRE.

THEN I GUESS YOU WON'T BE NEEDING THAT FREE UPGRADE.

IT'S ALL YOURS, PARTNER.

PLEASE, MAKE YOURSELVES COMFORTABLE. MS. COSOMATOS WILL BE WITH YOU IN A MOMENT.

LIEUTENANT GREER AND SERGEANT FORD WITH METRO POLICE. IS MR. CANTER HOME?
HE'S ON HOLIDAY UNTIL NEXT WEEK. IS THERE SOMETHING I CAN ASSIST YOU WITH?

IT'S URGENT THAT WE SPEAK WITH HIM. IS THERE A WAY HE CAN BE CONTACTED?
I'M AFRAID HE DIDN'T LEAVE ANY INSTRUCTIONS. HE CAN BE A VERY PRIVATE MAN.

IF YOU HEAR FROM HIM, PLEASE HAVE HIM CALL IMMEDIATELY. MY INFORMATION IS ON THE CARD.
OF COURSE, DETECTIVE.

IF YOU DON'T MIND MY ASKING . . . WAS HE IN SOME SORT OF ACCIDENT?
MR. CANTER SUFFERS FROM MOTOR NEURON DISEASE, A CONDITION THAT ATTACKS THE NERVOUS SYSTEM. IT'S LEFT HIM ALL BUT PARALYZED.

ANYONE ELSE WOULD'VE GIVEN UP WHEN THEY WERE DIAGNOSED, BUT MR. CANTER REFUSED TO LET HIS ILLNESS GET THE BETTER OF HIM.
HE CREATED THE SURROGATE SO THAT HE, AND OTHERS LIKE HIM, MIGHT HAVE A BETTER LIFE. HE'S QUITE AN INSPIRATION.

I SEE. THANK YOU FOR YOUR TIME.
I'M SORRY I COULDN'T BE MORE HELPFUL.

NOW I GET TO CALL THE COMMISSIONER AND TELL HIM THAT, IN SPITE OF LAST NIGHT'S EVENTS, WE *STILL* DON'T KNOW ANYTHING. THAT SHOULD BE FUN.
WE COULD FLY THE RECON PLANES OVER THE REZ. LOOK FOR STRUCTURES BIG ENOUGH TO HOUSE FACTORY EQUIPMENT.

NOT A BAD IDEA. AND HAVE RESEARCH TRY TO FIND CANTER. CHECK HIS CREDIT CARDS FOR AIRLINE AND HOTEL PURCHASES.
WE NEED TO TALK TO HIM, AND THE CLOCK IS RUNNING.
GOING DOWN.

NEWS RADIO, WGNU
HERE'S YOUR UPDATE AT THE TOP OF THE HOUR:

LAW ENFORCEMENT STILL HAS NO SUSPECT IN THE BREAK-IN LAST NIGHT AT CDV LABS.

DURING A PRESS CONFERENCE ON THE STEPS OF THE GOVERNMENT CENTER, METRO POLICE COMMISSIONER FREDERICK GRILLO HAD THIS TO SAY:

"THE DEPARTMENT IS FOLLOWING UP ON SEVERAL LEADS, AND WE'RE CONFIDENT THE PARTIES RESPONSIBLE WILL BE BROUGHT TO JUSTICE."

COMMISSIONER GRILLO WOULD NOT CONFIRM ANY LINK BETWEEN THE EVENTS AT CDV AND A SIMILAR CRIME THAT TOOK PLACE AT CLARK TECHNOLOGIES ON MAY 9.

AND IN OTHER NEWS . . .

FAITH, BROTHERS AND SISTERS.

FAITH HAS SUSTAINED YOU THROUGH ***PERSECUTION*** AND ***BANISHMENT***--

--AND IT IS FAITH THAT WILL CARRY YOU FORWARD WHEN THE EVE OF DARKEST NIGHT IS UPON YOU.

FOR MY TIME AMONG YOU HAS GROWN SHORT.

EVEN NOW, THOSE WHO HAVE ***REJECTED*** THE FATHER SEEK COUNSEL WITH ONE ANOTHER, PLOTTING FOR MY DEATH.

SO BE IT.
FOR WHEN THE ENEMIES OF GOD CONSPIRED AGAINST THE SON OF MAN, THEY DID NOT KNOW THAT THE END THEY SOUGHT WAS THEIR *OWN*--

INSTEAD TAKE COMFORT IN KNOWING THAT THE HOUR OF THE *LORD* IS AT HAND.

--AND THAT THE EVER-PRESENT HAND OF THE LORD GUIDED EVEN THEIR MOST *SECRET* ACTIONS.
NOTHING TRANSPIRES THAT *HE* HAS NOT SET IN MOTION.

AND WHEN AT LAST THE SHEPHERD IS STRUCK, DO NOT LET THE FLOCK BE SCATTERED.

MUSTER YOUR FAITH. MARCH ONWARD WITH THE SWORD OF *RIGHTEOUSNESS* DRAWN AND THE SHIELD OF *JUSTICE* PROTECTING YOU.

AND REMEMBER THAT I AM WITH YOU ALWAYS, EVEN UNTIL THE END OF THE AGE.

I KNEW THAT YOU WOULD COME.

IF IT IS POSSIBLE, LET THIS CUP PASS FROM ME--

--YET NOT MY WILL, BUT YOURS BE DONE.

YOUR EMINENCE, I HAVE RECEIVED THE EVENING'S REPORTS FROM THE STEWARDS.

YOUR EMIN--

ACOLYTE?

YES, MINISTER?
HAVE THE MASSES ASSEMBLED IMMEDIATELY.

THE *HOUR* IS AT HAND.

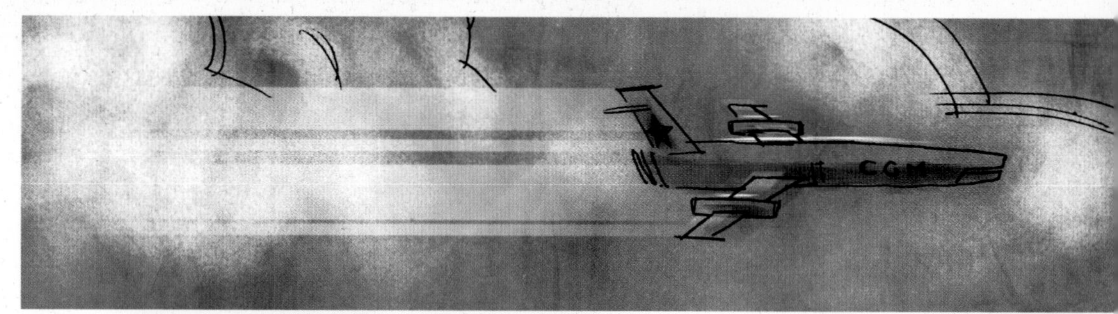

HAVEN'T WE DONE THIS ALREADY?

BRASS WANTED US TO MAKE A NIGHT RUN. IF THE DREADS HAVE A FACTORY DOWN THERE, THE SENSORS SHOULD PICK UP SOME HEAT BLOOMS.

HANG ON. THERMAL VISION IS BRINGING UP SOMETHING.

A FACTORY?
NEGATIVE.
LOOKS LIKE BIOLOGICS. ***THOUSANDS*** OF THEM.

LITTLE LATE FOR THE EVENING SERMON, ISN'T IT?
THAT'S WHAT I WAS THINKING.

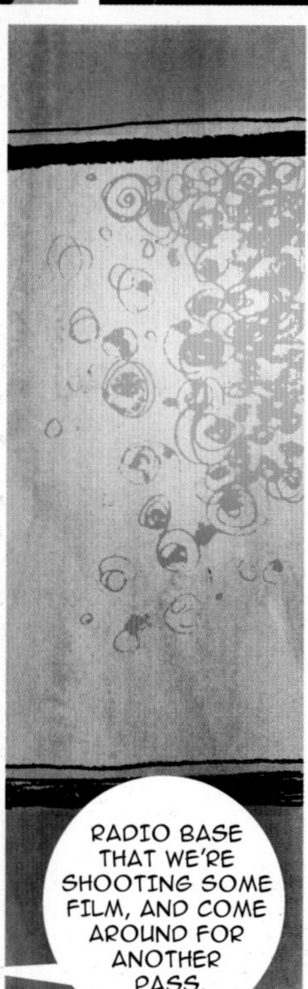
RADIO BASE THAT WE'RE SHOOTING SOME FILM, AND COME AROUND FOR ANOTHER PASS.

CHOOSE YOURSELF

LIFE...ONLY BETTER.

Designing the physical appearance of your surrogate is an important process, and our trained MODELING CONSULTANTS are ready to assist you. Using our state of the art facilities, they can replicate your current self, bring back an earlier self, or create a look for you that's entirely new. Whichever option you prefer, the result will be kept on file in our APPEARANCE DATABASE ensuring that the self you decide on will be yours and yours alone.

Once you've determined how your surrogate will look on the outside, you can leave the inside to us. Taking the field of cybernetics to a new level, our patented VIRTUAL SELF CHASSIS combines the durability of a machine with the grace and beauty of the human body. And because life shouldn't have to wait, every unit undergoes comprehensive testing to make certain that the power cells, circuitry, and mechanics will be ready to go whenever you are. We guarantee it for up to 5 years or 15,000 operating hours.*

Virtual Self is committed to providing you with a seamless living experience, and our VR LINK is what makes it all possible. This comfortable, lightweight headset turns your thoughts into real-time action, allowing your unit to perform as you would. Better, in fact, because with a surrogate you never have to worry about injury or fatigue. All you receive is sensory data so vivid, you'll know that you were there.

choose reliability
choose safety
choose freedom

unit options

Long-Life Power Cells	When you're on the go, finding time to recharge isn't always easy. Our Long-Life Power Cells lengthen the usage capacity of your unit to 150+ operating hours for each charge.
Reinforced Chassis	This structural upgrade is ideal for those who work or play on the edge. The reinforced design offers twice the tensile strength and impact resistance of our standard models.
SkinTough™	Another must for those in need of extra protection. The SkinTough™ sealant guards against punctures, tears, and soiling without compromising the lifelike look and texture of our cosmetic polymers.
Self-Cleaning Abdominal Reservoir	Cleanup is a snap with this modified reservoir. It uses chemicals to break down food and beverages into a disposable byproduct that's both convenient and environmentally safe.

software options

Data Recording & Playback	Why settle for memory alone? Use DRP to capture life's important moments. Whether it's the big game, your wedding day, or the birth of your child, you can relive the first time, every time.
Independent Motion	Everyone needs to step away from their surrogate once in a while. Independent Motion runs a sequence of programmed movements, giving your unit an animated appearance even when you're not linked.
Task Memory	Schedule your system to power down, run diagnostics, or perform other simple tasks. Task Memory does the remembering, so that you don't have to.
Forecast Manager™	Choose a set of climatic conditions, and your surrogate maintains them during any weather. With Forecast Manager™, every day is the perfect day.

system care

Customer Support*	In the event your surrogate experiences software or mechanical issues, you'll have access to our team of certified customer support technicians 24 hours a day, 7 days a week.
Extended Warranty*	Extend your surrogate's standard factory warranty to 10 years or 30,000 operating hours. Includes an annual 10-point inspection at any authorized Virtual Self dealership.

* All services and warranties are subject to Virtual Self's terms and conditions. Ask a Virtual Self representative for details.

FOR MORE INFORMATION,

VISIT A VIRTUAL SELF FACTORY SHOWROOM NEAR YOU

ATLANTA, GA
BALTIMORE, MD
BILLINGS, MT
BIRMINGHAM, AL
BOISE, ID
BOSTON, MA
CHARLESTON, SC
CHARLOTTE, NC
CHEYENNE, WY
CHICAGO, IL
CINCINNATI, OH
CLEVELAND, OH
DALLAS, TX
DENVER, CO
DES MOINES, IA
DETROIT, MI
FARGO, ND
HARTFORD, CT
HOUSTON, TX
INDIANAPOLIS, IN
JACKSON, MS
KANSAS CITY, MO
LAS VEGAS, NV
LOS ANGELES, CA
LOUISVILLE, KY
MANCHESTER, NH
MEMPHIS, TN
MIAMI, FL
MILWAUKEE, WI
NEW ORLEANS, LA
NEW YORK, NY
NEWARK, NJ
OKLAHOMA CITY, OK
OMAHA, NE
ORLANDO, FL
PHILADELPHIA, PA
PHOENIX, AZ
PITTSBURGH, PA
PORTLAND, OR
PROVIDENCE, RI
RICHMOND, VA
SAN ANTONIO, TX
SAN DIEGO, CA
SAN FRANCISCO, CA
SAN JOSE, CA
SANTA FE, NM
SEATTLE, WA
ST. LOUIS, MO
ST. PAUL, MN
TAMPA, FL
WICHITA, KS
WILMINGTON, DE

LIFE...ONLY BETTER.

chapter
FIVE

Pulse

MAY 14, 2054.
REC

WE'RE WORKING ON IT, COMMISSIONER. THERE'S AN EXPERT WHO CAN HELP US DETERMINE IF THE PROPHET'S BOOTLEGGING SURROGATES, BUT WE HAVEN'T BEEN ABLE TO TALK WITH HIM YET.

I'D HATE TO TAKE AWAY THE *ONE* NAME ON YOUR SUSPECT LIST, LIEUTENANT, BUT ZAIRE POWELL IS DEAD.
DEAD?

DEAD. INTEL ON THE GROUND IS SAYING SOMEONE SNUCK INTO HIS TENT LAST NIGHT AND ELECTROCUTED HIM.
SO, UNLESS YOU FIGURE PART OF THE PROPHET'S *GRAND SCHEME* WAS TO GET FRIED, I THINK IT'S TIME YOU FOCUSED YOUR INVESTIGATION ELSEWHERE.

I HAVE A DELIVERY FROM RESEARCH FOR LIEUTENANT GREER.
I'LL TAKE IT.
WHAT ABOUT XAVIER? MAYBE HE FINALLY GOT TIRED OF STANDING IN THE PROPHET'S SHAD--

LISTEN, HARVEY. IN LESS THAN *THREE HOURS*, THIS CITY'S GOING TO HAVE A RIOT ON ITS HANDS BIG ENOUGH TO MAKE THE LAST ONE LOOK LIKE A *PICNIC*, AND I STILL NEED TO BRIEF THE MAYOR.
I DON'T HAVE THE *TIME* OR THE *MANPOWER* TO BAIL YOU OUT.

SO I'M GIVING YOU FREE REIN. I DON'T CARE *WHAT* YOU HAVE TO DO, OR *WHO* YOU HAVE TO DO IT TO, JUST *DO* IT.
BUT IF YOU COME UP SHORT, MY NAME WON'T BE THE ONLY ONE GETTING TRASHED ON THE EVENING NEWS.

DAMN.

HARV, YOU NEED TO TAKE A LOOK AT THIS.
YOU KNOW WHY THE DREADS ARE COMING, PETE? BECAUSE LAST NIGHT SOMEBODY MURDERED THE PROPHET.

THAT'S RIGHT. ELECTROCUTED HIM. IMAGINE THAT.
WHICH MEANS THERE'S A GUY OUT THERE WITH HIS FINGER ON THE BUTTON, AND WE HAVE NO IDEA WHO OR WHERE HE IS.
HARV?

I DON'T HAVE TO TELL YOU WHAT WILL HAPPEN IF HE DISABLES OUR POLICE FORCE BEFORE IT CAN TURN BACK THE DREADS. WE HAVE LESS THAN THREE--
HARV!

GODDAMMIT, PETE! WHAT?

LOOK AT THIS.

IT'S FROM THE FILE RESEARCH PUT TOGETHER ON CANTER.

JESUS. DO YOU REALIZE WHAT THIS SAYS?

IT SAYS THAT WITHIN THE LAST SIX MONTHS, CANTER'S PROVIDED CONSULTING SERVICES FOR BOTH CLARK TECHNOLOGIES **AND** CDV LABS.
NOT A BAD GIG, IF YOU'RE TRYING TO CASE A LOCATION'S SECURITY.

THE PHOTOGRAPH.
WHAT?

THE PHOTOGRAPH I SAW AT CANTER'S PENTHOUSE. HE WAS IN A WHEELCHAIR.
I'M NOT FOLLOWING YOU.

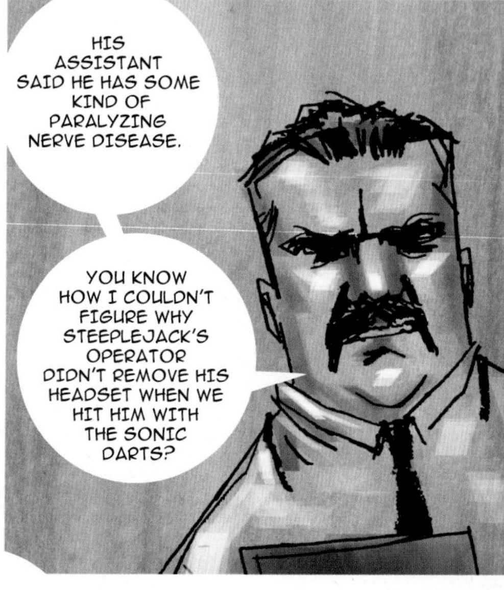
HIS ASSISTANT SAID HE HAS SOME KIND OF PARALYZING NERVE DISEASE.
YOU KNOW HOW I COULDN'T FIGURE WHY STEEPLEJACK'S OPERATOR DIDN'T REMOVE HIS HEADSET WHEN WE HIT HIM WITH THE SONIC DARTS?

YEAH.
WELL, HOW'S A GUY WITH A CONDITION LIKE THAT SUPPOSED TO REMOVE HIS HEADSET?

HE COULDN'T. HE'D HAVE TO FIND A WAY TO FIGHT THROUGH THE NOISE. IS THAT EVEN POSSIBLE?
APPARENTLY.
WE NEED TO MAKE SOME CALLS.

MAYOR
ARTHUR
FELDSTEIN

WITH THE USE OF SATELLITE SURVEILLANCE, MR. MAYOR, WE'VE ESTIMATED THE SIZE OF THE DREAD FORCE TO BE ROUGHLY EIGHTY THOUSAND MEN AND WOMEN.

IF WE PULL MOST OF THE PATROLMEN OFF OF THEIR BEATS AND GO TO MINIMUM CAPACITY AT ALL OF THE PRECINCTS--
--WE CAN HAVE TWENTY-TWO THOUSAND OFFICERS AT THE CITY'S EDGE WITHIN TWO HOURS.

THE NATIONAL GUARD IS MOBILIZING ANOTHER TEN THOUSAND FROM FORT MACPHERSON, AND WE CAN DEPLOY ENOUGH RESERVE TRUCKS TO MAKE UP THE DIFFERENCE.
WE'LL HAVE BETTER EQUIPMENT AND TRAINING, BUT AGAINST A MOB THIS SIZE? IT COULD BE DAYS BEFORE WE KNOW THE OUTCOME.

WHAT ARE YOU SAYING, FRED?
I'M SAYING WE NEED TO OPEN UP THE ARSENAL.

USE *LIVE* AMMUNITION? AGAINST *PEOPLE*?

I DON'T SEE THAT WE HAVE AN OPTION. AS WE SPEAK, SOMEONE IS ASSEMBLING A WEAPON THAT CAN TURN OUR ENTIRE FORCE INTO ONE GIANT SCRAP HEAP.
THIS UPRISING HAS TO BE PUT DOWN QUICKLY AND DECISIVELY, *BEFORE* THAT HAS A CHANCE TO HAPPEN. IF IT ISN'T, THE DREADS WILL RUN UNCHECKED THROUGH THE CITY.

HOW DID WE GET TO THIS?
THE PROBLEM WITH AN ACHILLES HEEL IS THAT YOU DON'T KNOW IT'S THERE UNTIL SOMEONE STRIKES IT.

WE NEVER CONSIDERED THE POSSIBILITY THAT EMP TECHNOLOGY MIGHT BE USED AGAINST US.
THERE HASN'T BEEN ENOUGH TIME TO FORMULATE A CONTINGENCY PLAN SHOULD OUR SURROGATE OFFICERS BECOME INCAPACITATED.

WHERE ARE ALL OF THE REAL COPS? CAN'T WE CALL THEM IN?
SURE, IF YOU WANT TO FIELD A FORCE OF PTA MOMMIES AND OLD MEN.

TWELVE YEARS AGO, WE HAD THE HIGHEST CRIME RATE IN THE NATION. WE SWITCHED TO AN ALL-SURROGATE POLICE FORCE--A REFERENDUM YOU CAMPAIGNED ON--

--WITH THE HOPE THAT A SAFE WORK ENVIRONMENT AND LESS PHYSICAL DEMANDS WOULD DRAW MORE PEOPLE TO THE DEPARTMENT.
WELL, IT WORKED, AND THE CRIME RATE DROPPED TO NOTHING.

EXCEPT NOW THERE AREN'T MANY OFFICERS ON OUR PAYROLL CAPABLE OF DOING THE JOB WITHOUT A STAND-IN. THERE CERTAINLY AREN'T ENOUGH TO SEND A MOB THIS SIZE PACKING.

LIVE ROUNDS MIGHT NOT BE THE IDEAL SOLUTION, BUT IT'S THE BEST WE'VE GOT.
GOD HELP US.

I UNDERSTAND, SIR.

LOCKER RO

OKAY, EVERYBODY. LISTEN UP.

THE MAYOR HAS AUTHORIZED THE USE OF LIVE AMMUNITION.
AFTER YOU RECEIVE YOUR ASSIGNMENTS, REPORT TO THE ARMORY FOR RESUPPLY.

WHEN'S THE LAST TIME YOU FIRED A *REAL* BULLET, CARTER?

NOT SINCE THE ACADEMY.
I HAVEN'T FIRED ONE SINCE THE *LAST* RIOT, BUT YOU CAN TAKE IT FROM ME--

--WHEN YOU SEE WHAT THE DREADS ARE CAPABLE OF, YOU'LL BE *GLAD* TO HAVE SOMETHING BESIDES SCREAMERS IN YOUR CHAMBER.

ARE WE READY TO BROADCAST? THEY'LL BE COMING THROUGH ANY SECOND.

WE'RE HOT.
OKAY, WHEN THEY'RE CLOSE ENOUGH, GET A SHOT OF ME WITH THE CROWD IN THE BACKGROUND.

HERE THEY COME.

ROLLING.
I'M DONNA REID WITH GNN HEADLINE NEWS, AND WE'RE STANDING ON INTERSTATE SEVENTY-FIVE, JUST SOUTH OF CENTRAL GEORGIA METROPOLIS.
REC

BEHIND ME, AN ARMY OF DREADS MARCHES TOWARD THE CITY IN RESPONSE TO THE MURDER OF THEIR LEADER, ZAIRE POWELL III, ALSO KNOWN AS THE PROPHET.

THIS MOB'S INTENTIONS ARE UNCLEAR, BUT AS ITS MEMBERS BRANDISH CLUBS, KNIVES, AND EVEN GUNS, ONE CAN ONLY ASSUME THAT THIS IS NOT A PEACEFUL DEMONSTRATION.
LET'S ASK ONE OF THE PARTICIPANTS.

MISS? CAN YOU TELL US WHAT YOU PLAN TO DO WHEN YOU REACH THE CITY?
ABOMINATION!

AND JUST LIKE THAT, DONNA'S ON VACATION.
YEAH, RIGHT. A LEAD ANCHOR LIKE HER? YOU ***KNOW*** THE NETWORK HAS HER APPEARANCE TRADEMARKED. I BET A DOUBLE'S ALREADY LEAVING THE STATION.
GNN

GET THE EQUIPMENT TOGETHER, SCREWS. AND STAY BY THE PHONE.

WHAT'D YOU FIND OUT?
I TALKED TO CANTER'S ASSISTANT, AND YOU WERE RIGHT. HE DOES HAVE A SURRIE WITH HIM, BUT GET THIS--

--IT'S NOT JUST ANY SURRIE. IT'S THE *FIRST* ONE-- THE PROTOTYPE HE DEVELOPED THAT BECAME THE FORERUNNER OF THEM ALL. VSI GAVE IT TO HIM AS A RETIREMENT GIFT.

AND SINCE IT PREDATES THE MASS PRODUCTION OF SURROGATES, ITS PARTS WOULDN'T HAVE VINS.
RIGHT. BUT IT *HAS* TO HAVE A SIGNAL ADDRESS, OR ELSE IT WOULDN'T WORK. SO LET'S GET VSI TO TERMINATE IT-- CUT TRANSMISSION AT THE SOURCE.

WHAT IF HE HAS A BACKUP UNIT? HE COULD RE-LINK AND NOT MISS A BEAT.
AS I SEE IT, THE ONLY WAY TO STOP CANTER IS TO *FIND* HIM. I'D RATHER USE THE SIGNAL FOR THAT.

SCREWS SAYS HE CAN PINPOINT AN OPERATOR'S GEOGRAPHIC POSITION BY TRIANGULATING THE TRANSMISSION SIGNAL, BUT HE'LL NEED THE SIGNAL ADDRESS.
VSI MUST HAVE IT ON RECORD. YOU HEAD DOWN THERE AND TALK TO WELCH. HE'LL SAY YOU CAN'T HAVE IT WITHOUT A WARRANT, BUT *DON'T LEAVE* WITHOUT THAT ADDRESS.

WHAT ARE *YOU* GOING TO DO?
DON'T WORRY ABOUT ME. JUST MAKE SURE HE GIVES IT TO YOU.

MR. WELCH DOES **NOT** WANT TO BE DISTURBED.

I APOLOGIZE, MR. WELCH, BUT HE WOULDN'T LISTEN TO ME.

IT'S ALRIGHT, GINNY. YOU CAN GO BACK TO YOUR DESK.

REALLY, SERGEANT. I KNOW I SAID I'D HELP IN ANY WAY THAT I COULD, BUT I SIMPLY **CANNOT** BE AT YOUR BECK AND CALL.

I UNDERSTAND, BUT I DON'T HAVE TIME TO MAKE AN APPOINTMENT.
VERY WELL.
WHAT IS IT THAT YOU NEED?

WHEN LIONEL CANTER RETIRED, YOU LET HIM HAVE THE PROTOTYPE SURROGATE. I NEED ITS SIGNAL ADDRESS.

CERTAINLY. I CAN GET THAT INFORMATION FOR YOU JUST AS SOON AS I SEE A WARRANT.

I DON'T HAVE A WARRANT.
THEN I SUGGEST YOU COME BACK WHEN YOU DO.

THERE'S NO TIME. IN CASE YOU HAVEN'T HEARD, THERE'S AN ARMY OF DREADS MARCHING ON THE CITY.
YES, I SAW WHAT THEY DID TO THAT REID WOMAN. HOW *TERRIBLE*.

I SYMPATHIZE WITH YOU, SERGEANT. I REALLY DO. BUT AN OPERATOR'S ANONYMITY IS THE ***CORNERSTONE*** OF THE SURROGATE EXPERIENCE.

TO BREACH THAT CODE OF CONFIDENTIALITY WOULD SIMPLY BE ***UNETHICAL***, AND IT WOULD EXPOSE VSI TO HARSH LITIGATION.
I'M SURE YOU UNDERSTAND.

THAT'S NOT GOOD ENOUGH, WELCH. BY WITHHOLDING THAT INFORMATION, YOU'RE PUTTING THE CITY IN DANGER.
THAT SOUNDS LIKE A MATTER FOR THE POLICE DEPARTMENT.

I'M NOT GOING TO ASK AGAIN.
ARE YOU GOING TO ***BEAT*** THE INFORMATION OUT OF ME, SERGEANT? YOUR INSTINCT MAY BE TO SETTLE THIS WITH PHYSICALITY--

--BUT, GIVEN THE CIRCUMSTANCES, I'M SURE YOU REALIZE THE FUTILITY OF THAT COURSE OF ACTION.

TURN AROUND. SLOWLY.

YOU'RE VICTOR WELCH?

VICTORIA, ACTUALLY.
THE BOARD OF DIRECTORS FEELS MORE SECURE HAVING A MALE CEO. INVESTORS LIKE THAT SORT OF THING.

IT'S A MAN'S WORLD.

NOT ANYMORE.

SO, YOU THINK LIONEL IS THE PERSON YOU'RE LOOKING FOR?
I MUST ADMIT, I'M NOT SURPRISED. HIS RETIREMENT FROM VSI WASN'T ENTIRELY VOLUNTARY.

YOU SEE, HE CONCEIVED THE SURROGATE TO BE AN ELABORATE PROSTHETIC, AND NEVER SUPPORTED ANY USE OF THE TECHNOLOGY BEYOND THAT PURPOSE.
AS A CORPORATION, HOWEVER, IT'S OUR JOB TO MARKET OUR PRODUCTS AS AGGRESSIVELY AS POSSIBLE.

WHEN THE BOARD MADE ITS DECISION TO FINALLY GO AFTER THE UNDER-EIGHTEEN DEMOGRAPHIC, LIONEL'S WAS THE LONE DISSENTING VOICE.
HE FELT THAT THE WIDESPREAD USE OF SURROGATES AMONG ADULTS WAS BAD ENOUGH, BUT AMONG CHILDREN . . . THAT WAS MORE THAN HE COULD ACCEPT.

HE BEGAN ESPOUSING VSI'S MORAL AND ETHICAL RESPONSIBILITY TO REGULATE THE USE OF SURROGATES, AND RIGHT THEN WE KNEW IT WAS TIME FOR HIM TO GO.
TO HAVE SUCH A VOCAL OPPONENT OCCUPY ONE OF THE COMPANY'S TOP POSITIONS SIMPLY WOULDN'T BE GOOD BUSINESS.

SO YOU ASKED HIM TO RETIRE, AND HE AGREED--BUT ONLY IF YOU LET HIM HAVE THE PROTOTYPE.

IT SEEMED A SMALL PRICE FOR AVOIDING THE SCANDAL OF FIRING SUCH A HIGH-PROFILE RESEARCHER. THE PROTOTYPE HAD BECOME LITTLE MORE THAN A COMPANY SHOWPIECE, AND WE WOULD'VE GLADLY GIVEN HIM SO MUCH MORE.

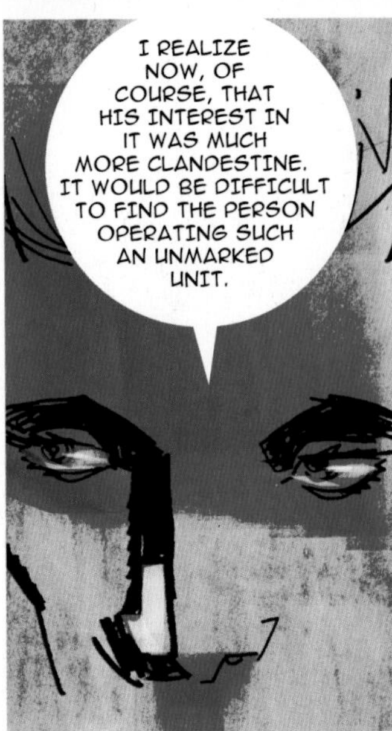
I REALIZE NOW, OF COURSE, THAT HIS INTEREST IN IT WAS MUCH MORE CLANDESTINE. IT WOULD BE DIFFICULT TO FIND THE PERSON OPERATING SUCH AN UNMARKED UNIT.

BUT NOT IMPOSSIBLE. WE NEED THAT SIGNAL ADDRESS. IF WE DON'T FIND CANTER SOON, WE'RE ALL GOING TO TAKE A TWENTY-YEAR TUMBLE INTO THE PAST.

I ASSUME YOU'RE REFERRING TO LIONEL'S ACQUISITION OF THE EMP DEVICE?

DON'T LOOK SO SHOCKED, LIEUTENANT. THANKS TO THE LARGE NUMBER OF CORPORATE SPIES ON OUR PAYROLL, THERE'S NOTHING VSI ISN'T PRIVY TO.
LAW ENFORCEMENT COULD LEARN MUCH FROM THE WAY WE DO THINGS.

TELL ME. WHY SHOULD I HELP YOU?
LEGALLY, I'M OBLIGATED NOT TO. AND FROM A BUSINESS STANDPOINT--

--WELL, WHAT YOU CONSIDER TO BE A TRAGEDY SOUNDS TO ME LIKE MILLIONS OF REPEAT CUSTOMERS.

YOU DON'T GET IT, DO YOU, WELCH?
CANTER USED US ALL.

HE USED ME TO GET TO THE PROPHET. HE USED THE PROPHET TO DRAW ATTENTION FROM HIMSELF.

AND HE'S USING YOU TO HELP HIM FINISH HIS PLAN.
DO YOU THINK THAT ONCE HE RELEASES THE EMP, ALL OF THOSE DREADS WILL JUST MARCH HOME? OR WILL THEY CONTINUE TO YOUR FACTORY AND BURN IT TO THE GROUND?

IT'LL BE HARD TO SATISFY ALL OF THOSE REPEAT CUSTOMERS WITHOUT A PRODUCTION FACILITY.
FACTORIES CAN BE REBUILT. THE INTERIM WILL ONLY REMIND OPERATORS HOW MUCH THEY'VE COME TO DEPEND ON THEIR UNITS.

SURROGATES HAVE SOUNDED THE DEATH KNELL OF THE OLD WORLD. THAT BELL CANNOT BE UNRUNG.

AND WHAT ABOUT YOU? WILL YOUR CUSTOMERS TRUST A COMPANY LED BY SOMEONE WHO MIGHT'VE PREVENTED THE DESTRUCTION?
YOU'LL BE THE ONE WHO LET THEM DOWN.

I'LL DENY THIS MEETING, OF COURSE, AND THEY'LL BELIEVE ME BECAUSE THEY ***WANT*** TO.

ARE YOU SURE THE BOARD OF DIRECTORS--THE SAME BOARD THAT'S SO PARTICULAR ABOUT VSI'S IMAGE IT INSISTS THAT YOU BE A MAN--WILL RISK IT?

YOU WON'T STOP HIM. LIONEL IS NOTHING IF NOT CLEVER.
BUT I DON'T HAVE TO TELL YOU THAT, DO I, LIEUTENANT?
I'LL TAKE MY CHANCES.

VERY WELL . . . NOW ***YOU*** CAN BE THE ONE WHO LET EVERYONE DOWN.

YOU DON'T GET TO BE CEO BY BEING ONE WHO'S EASILY BESTED, SERGEANT. YOUR PARTNER IS QUITE RESOURCEFUL.
I'LL NEED A MOMENT TO ACCESS THE INFORMATION.

YOU HAVE A CALL.

I GUESS I KNOW WHERE YOU ARE.

PICK UP SCREWS AND HAVE HIM START THE TRACE. HE CAN TALK ME IN FROM YOUR END.
AND ROUND UP WHOEVER YOU CAN GET FROM THE PRECINCT.

GIVE LIONEL MY BEST.

SURE THING. I HOPE YOU DON'T MIND MY BORROWING YOUR PEN.

NOT AT ALL . . .

POLICE

DO NOT FALTER, BROTHERS AND SISTERS.

FEAR NO HARM, FOR THE ***LORD*** IS WITH US.
HE WILL MAKE HIMSELF ***KNOWN*** IN THE PRESENCE OF OUR ***ENEMIES***.

SO SAYETH THE PSALM.

THERE'S HARV.

YOU'RE SURE HE'S IN THERE?
IT'S SIMPLE TRIANGULATION. GEOMETRY DOESN'T LIE.

THERE! ON THE ROOF!

I NEED ONE PATROLMAN WITH ME AND SCREWS.
EVERYONE ELSE HEAD TO THE ROOF WITH SERGEANT FORD.

THE SCREAMERS WON'T WORK AT FIRST, BUT KEEP HITTING HIM.
THE GUY'S *GOT* TO HAVE A BREAKING POINT.

THIS IS IT.

LET'S GIVE THE DREADS A CHANCE TO TURN BACK--

--BUT IF THEY DON'T TAKE IT, EVERYONE FIRE ON MY COMMAND.

JUST A COUPLE MORE FLIGHTS.

INSERT DISC...

FREQUENCY TARGETED
PULSE READY

FIRE.

STREICHER
lager

18 FT

HERE THEY COME.

THIS IS WHAT YOU WANTED. YOU'VE CHANGED THE WORLD BACK.
BUT FOR HOW LONG?

MAYBE WELCH IS RIGHT. MAYBE THE BELL CAN'T BE UNRUNG, AND THE WHOLE THING WILL START ALL OVER AGAIN.

MAYBE NOT. NOW WE WAIT AND SEE.
BUT YOU DON'T PLAN TO BE AROUND THAT LONG, DO YOU?

THERE REALLY ISN'T ANY POINT IN TAKING YOU IN. WASTING AWAY IN THAT CHAIR IS WORSE THAN ANY SENTENCE THE PENAL CODE COULD IMPOSE.

END IT THE WAY YOU WANT. YOU'VE DONE YOUR BEST TO SQUARE THE BOOKS, SO I SUPPOSE I OWE YOU THAT MUCH.

AND ME?
WELL, SOMEBODY FROM THE DEPARTMENT IS GOING TO TAKE THE FALL--

--SO I DON'T THINK I'LL BE NEEDING THIS ANYMORE.

YOU KEEP IT. MY HEART WOULDN'T BE IN IT ANYWAY.

I GUESS THAT'S IT THEN.

NEWS RADIO, WGNU

THE DREADS HAVE STOPPED THEIR MARCH AT THE FACTORY COMPLEX OF VIRTUAL SELF, INCORPORATED, AND THE BUILDING HAS BEEN RAZED.

THE VSI HOME OFFICE TOWER IS ALSO IN FLAMES, AND THE CORPORATE MAINFRAMES HAVE BEEN DESTROYED. REPORTS OF SURROGATE OPERATIONS FAILURES ARE COMING IN FROM ACROSS THE NATION.

LOCALLY, WITNESSES ARE REPORTING THAT THE DREADS ARE MAKING NO THREATS TOWARD THE GENERAL POPULATION, AND ARE INSTEAD ORGANIZING A MASSIVE SURROGATE CLEANUP CAMPAIGN.

THEY INVITE ALL WHO ARE WILLING TO JOIN THEM IN THIS EFFORT, AS THEY INTEND TO WITHDRAW FROM THE CITY ONCE THE CLEANUP IS CONCLUDED.

THERE'S BEEN NO WORD AS TO WHEN PUBLIC SERVICES AND REGULAR MEDIA BROADCASTING WILL RESUME--

--BUT CITY OFFICIALS ARE ASKING THAT ALL ABLE-BODIED CITIZENS REPORT TO THEIR PLACES OF EMPLOYMENT AS SOON AS POSSIBLE.

THOSE UNABLE TO PERFORM IN THEIR CURRENT JOBS SHOULD CONTACT THE LABOR BUREAU FOR REASSIGNMENT.

STAY TUNED FOR CONTINUING REPORTS.

MARGARET?

IT'S OVER, MARGARET. PEOPLE ARE STARTING TO COME OUT OF THEIR BUILDINGS.
I THOUGHT MAYBE WE COULD GO FOR A WALK.

OPEN THE DOOR, MARGARET.

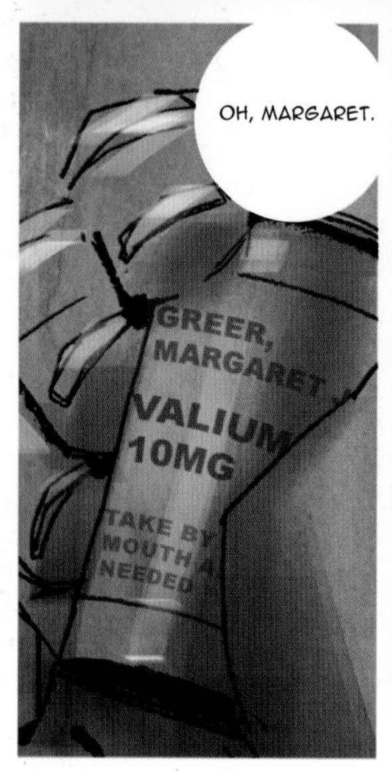
OH, MARGARET.
GREER, MARGARET
VALIUM 10MG
TAKE BY MOUTH A NEEDED

END

COVERS GALLERY

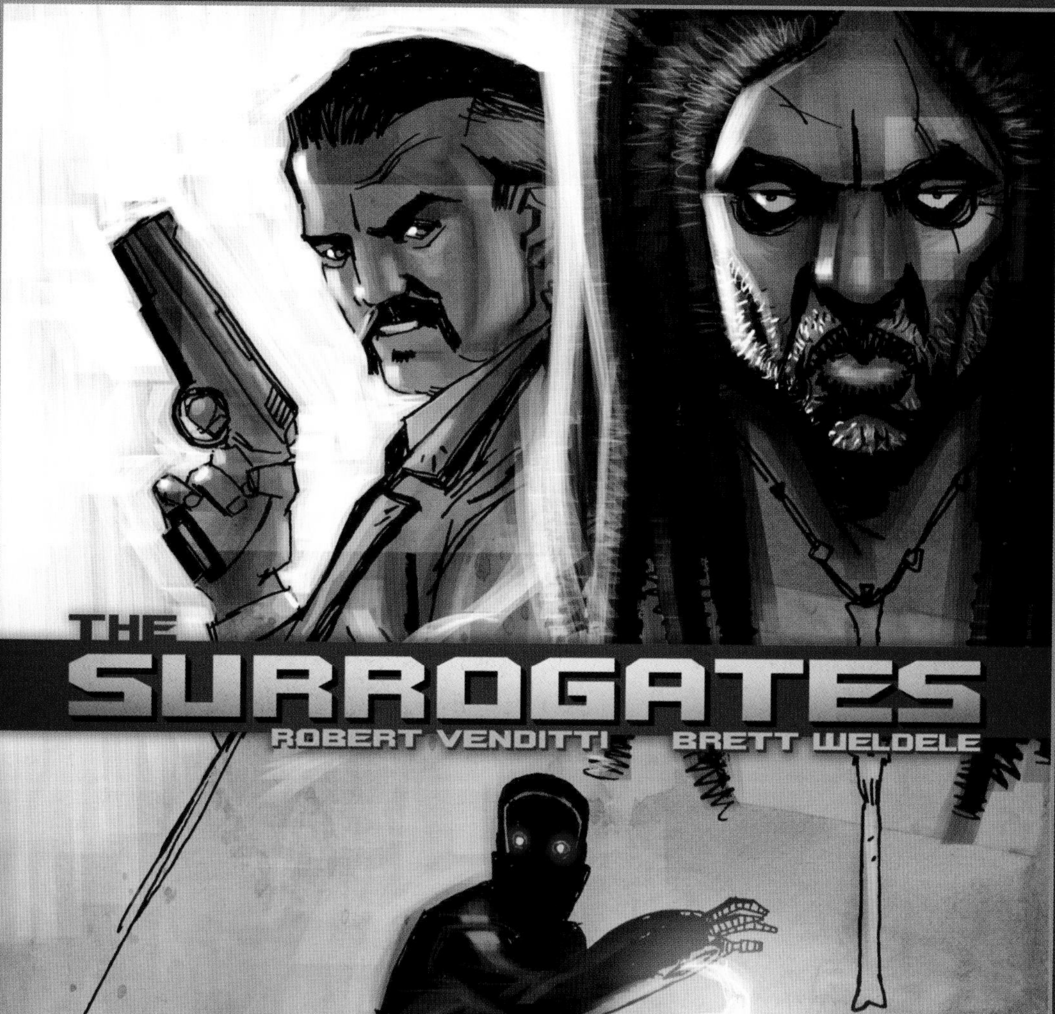

issue
ONE

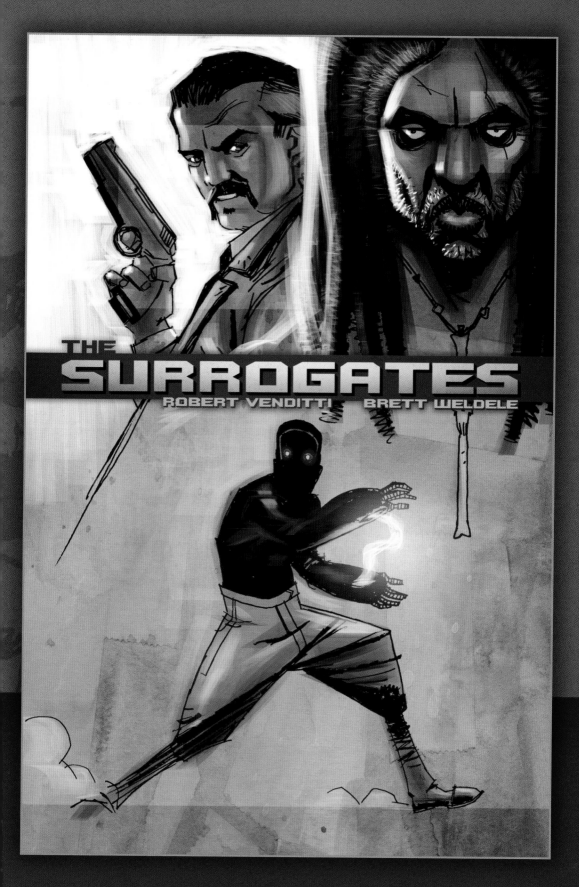

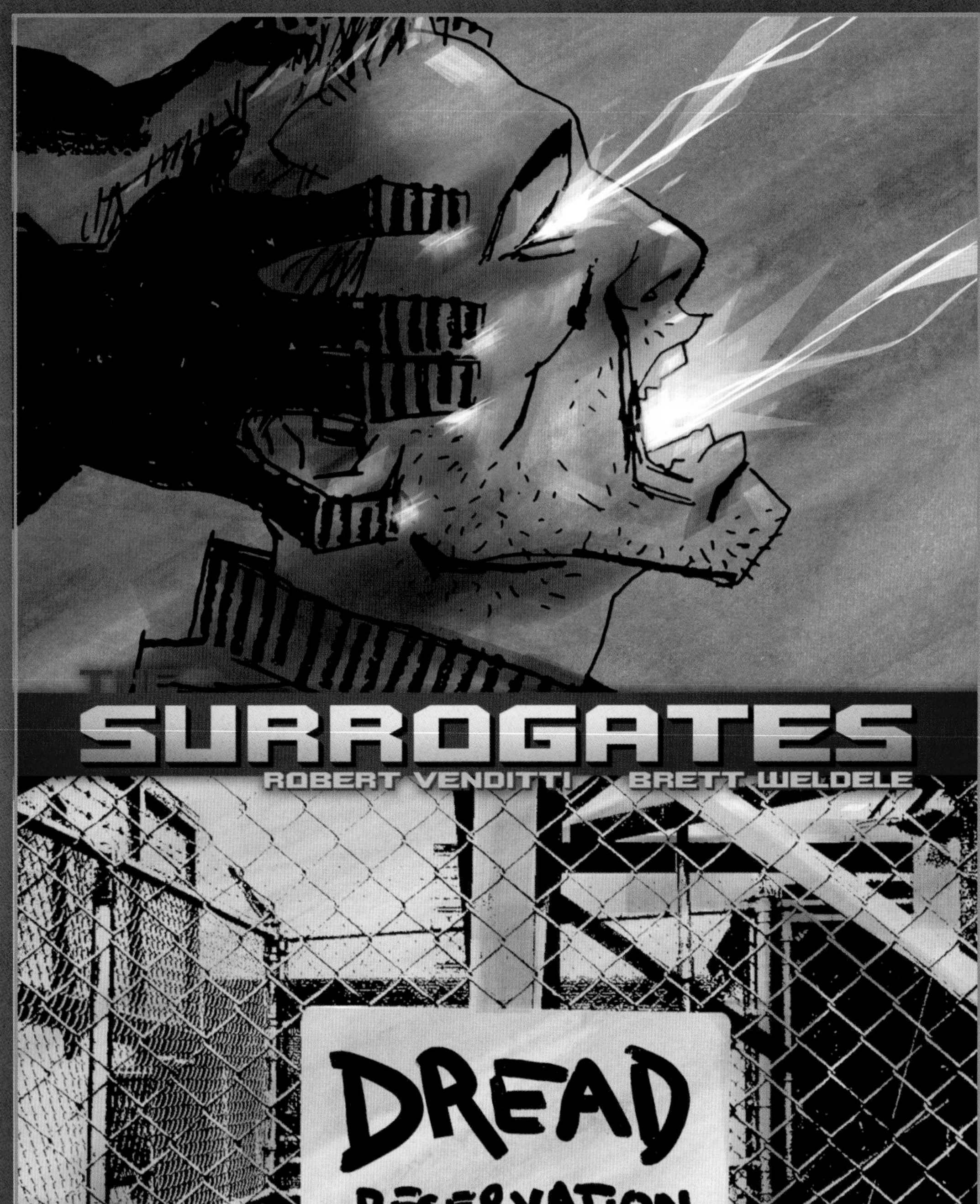
SURROGATES
ROBERT VENDITTI
BRETT WELDELE
DREAD
RESERVATION

issue

TWO

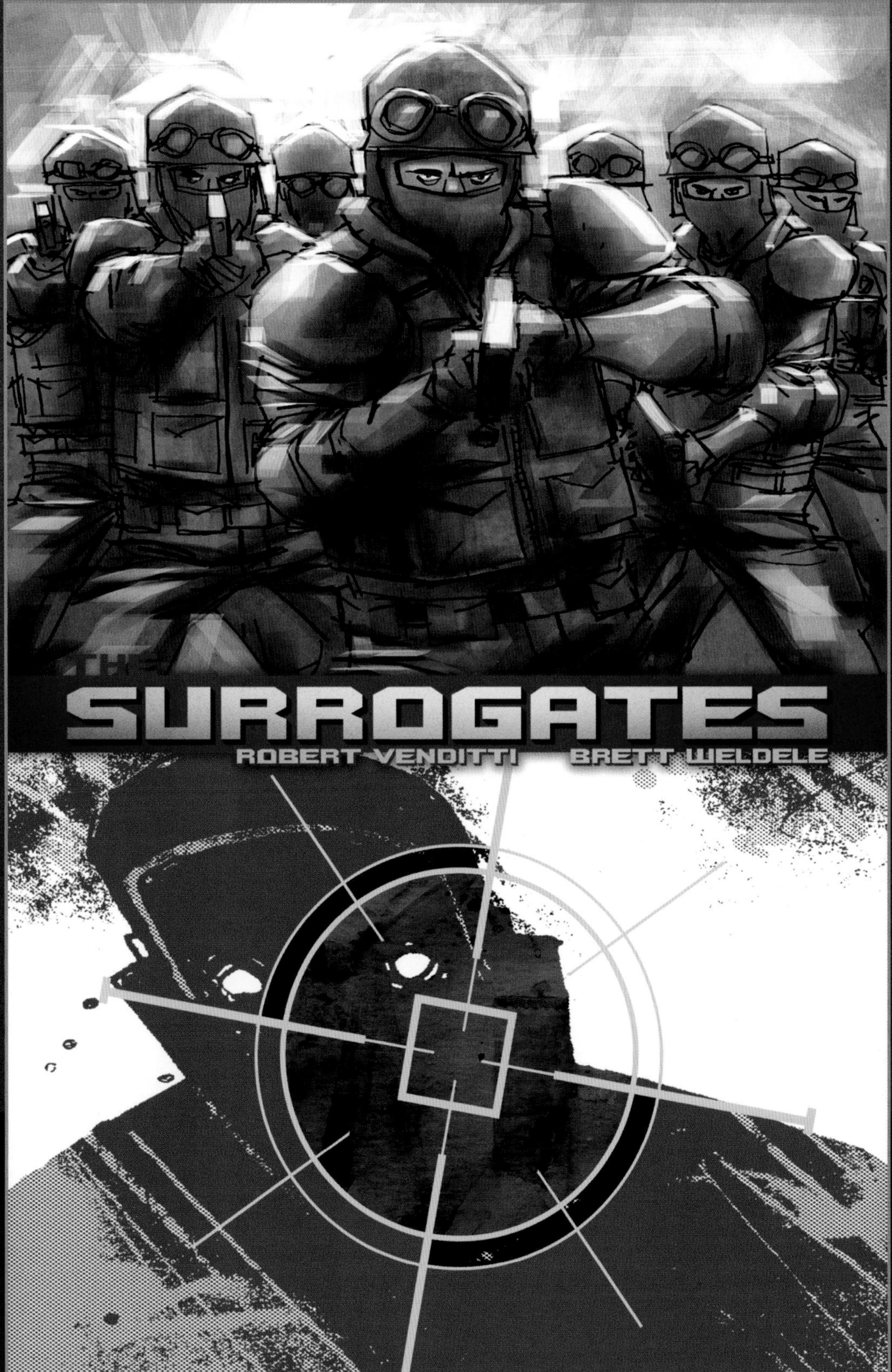

issue
THREE

THE

SURROGATES

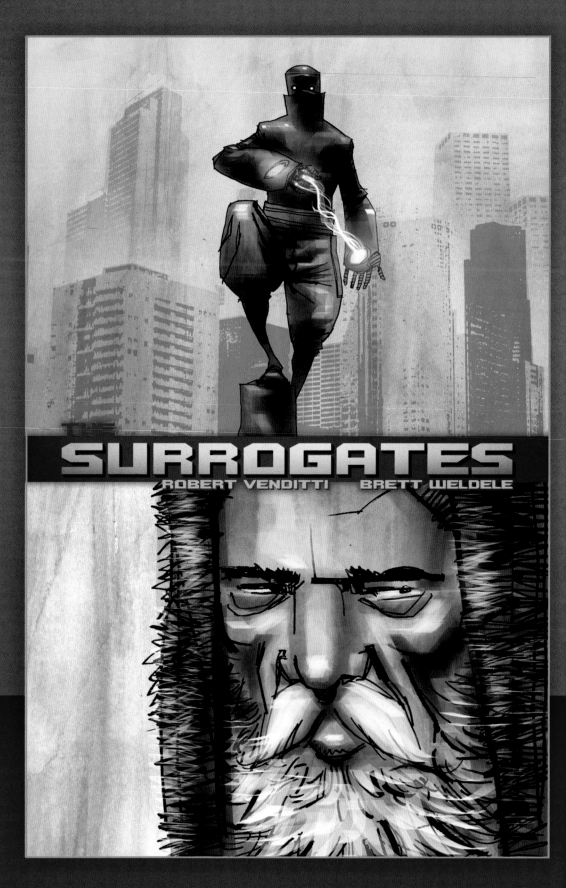

ROBERT VENDITTI BRETT WELDELE

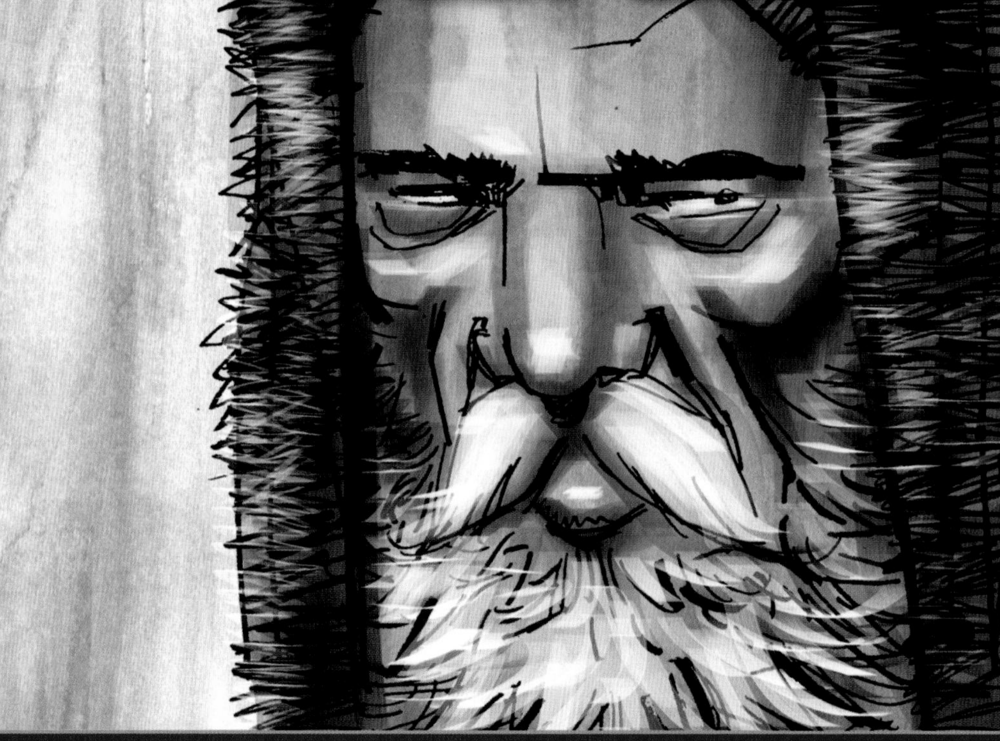

issue
FOUR

THE SURROGATES

ROBERT VENDITTI BRETT WELDELE

issue
FIVE

Deciding I wanted to write comics for a living was easy. Learning how to go about it . . . not so much. In 2002, when I began to seriously entertain the idea of a career in comics, a careful search of the section titled "Writing for Publication" at my local Borders yielded an inexhaustible supply of books about the keys to writing successful romance novels or the ten easy steps to crafting mysteries that sell, but not much about the nuts and bolts of comics. So for the most part I was left to read my collected editions of *Astro City* and *Watchmen* and wonder how on earth they ever came to exist.

Today the situation is a little better—from what I hear, there's even a *Complete Idiot's Guide to Creating a Graphic Novel*—but what I eventually came to find out was that there's no tried-and-true method, no universal recipe for getting the comic books out of your head and onto someone else's shelf. As Screws would say, "You don't bake them in an oven." There are as many ways to make comics as there are people who make them.

This is a look at how we made this one.

— ROBERT VENDITTI

THE SURROGATES

BEHIND THE SCENES

FROM CONCEPT TO PAGE

THIS IS AN EXCERPT FROM MY ORIGINAL CHARACTER DESCRIPTION FOR THE PROPHET AND BRETT'S CORRESPONDING CONCEPTUAL DESIGN.

"The Prophet is worn and battle-scarred, but his wiry body is taut from hard living. He has dark skin, long, black dreadlocks, a black scraggly beard, and wears no shirt (he never wears a shirt, only tattered pants with a rope belt and sandals). A necklace hangs around his neck with a cross made of bone. There is an ugly scar that cuts across his left eye and cheek. He carries a twisted staff at all times, a symbol of his leadership and power."

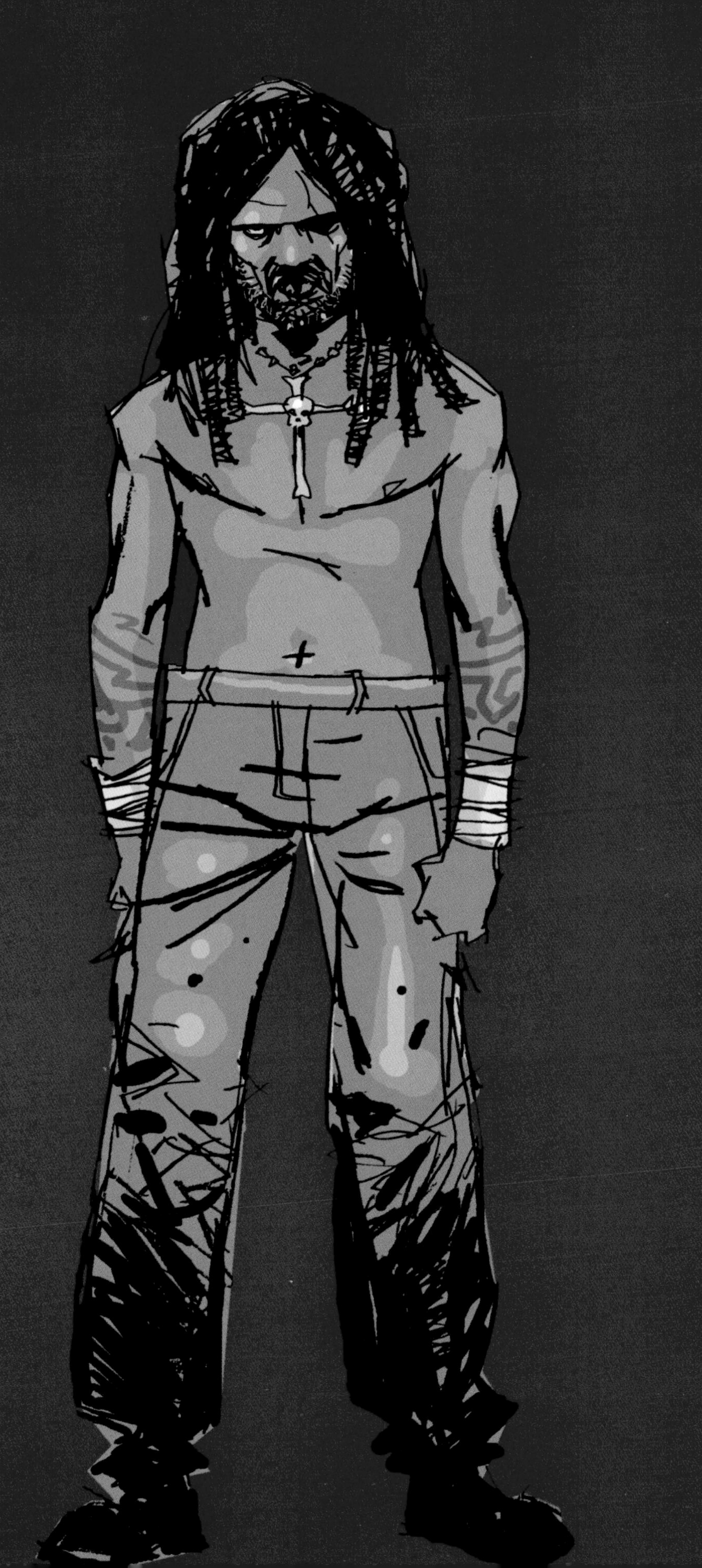

FOR STEEPLEJACK, BRETT ADDED SUCH ELEMENTS AS THE FACEGUARD AND GAUNTLETS, TURNING AN OTHERWISE GENERIC DESCRIPTION INTO A COMPELLING CHARACTER.

“SteepleJack travels via the city’s rooftops, lowering himself to and raising himself from the ground with guns that fire thin but extremely sturdy cable. He is tall and muscular, but not overly so—more athletic than massive. Whenever we see him without his clothes he is completely hairless, and his muscles are well-defined. He dresses in a black duster and heavy black boots, and wears black goggles over his eyes. Beneath his clothes is a black bodysuit that covers him head to toe, so that none of his skin is visible.”

SCRIPT TO PAGE

From the time I started writing the first script until the time the last issue hit the stands, *The Surrogates* was nearly four years in the making. The next several pages show the steps the story went through as it was translated from script to finished page. I chose this scene from Chapter 5 as an example because it's the moment that the entire series has been building up to—Harvey finally gets his man, but the outcome is much different than anticipated. Also, I've discovered that subdued character interactions are far more difficult to pull off than fast-paced action sequences.

It's worth pointing out that often in comics there's a separate penciller, inker, colorist, and letterer to perform each step in the art process. It's a testament to Brett's abilities that he can handle all of these tasks himself.

CHAPTER 5 / PAGE 28 (8 Panels)

PANEL 1: Harvey's view through the open apartment door of Canter's wheelchair. He is centered in front of a window—make the window large enough that Harvey can stand next to Canter in Panel 3 and still be in front of it—and the chair is turned away from us so that we see the back of it. He and the window are in turn centered in the open doorway. The blinds are raised from the window. The window is not across from another housing unit, but looks over the street, so there is a fair amount of sunlight landing on Canter and casting a long shadow behind him. There are no other lights on in the room, nor can we see any other furnishings. We cannot see Canter sitting in the wheelchair because the chair is large—designed with comfort in mind as well as mobility—and Canter's condition has reduced him to a shrunken-down state. We can see the computer that operates his VR link, however, fastened to the back of the chair so that it can be mobile as well. There are battery backups attached to the back of the chair to keep the unit running during transit or power outages, and the cables that connect the computer to the VR link are bound by Velcro strips to the chair's metal supports—this would keep the cables from snagging on something while the chair is in motion. There is a handle with a rubber grip at each of the chair's top corners so someone can walk behind the chair and push it. We may be too far away to see the cables and Velcro, but keep it in mind for future panels as I think it needs to be addressed.

PANEL 2: Canter from the front, sitting in his chair. We are close in, so we see him from the stomach up. This is the first time we have seen him, and I would like to communicate in this panel all of the fragility and desperation that drove the character to choose the path he did. His condition makes his age hard to guess, but, for the record, Canter is in his early-fifties, making Harvey his contemporary. He wears a long-sleeved, button-down shirt and slacks, though we cannot see his pants in this panel. His hands lay in his lap—again, we cannot see the hands because they are below panel bottom, but position his arms in such a way that we understand his hands are in his lap. He is nestled into his wheelchair, which is cushioned and comfortable looking. He wears a standard VR link, but has fashioned a strap device that holds it securely on his head—after all, if the VR link were to fall off, SteepleJack would cease to work, and Canter would be REALLY screwed. The straps go under his chin and around the back of his head, bunching his hair goofily in places. Canter's eyes are concentrated on the window, which is off-panel behind us.

PANEL 3: Harvey is now standing beside Canter's chair. This is a profile of them both with Harvey in the foreground, but we are angled slightly to the right so Canter is not hidden behind Harvey. We see Harvey from the waist up and at his level, so there is a slight down shot to Canter that shows his hands laying palms-up in his lap. Harvey's hands are in his pockets. Both men are looking out the window, Harvey's head angled down so he can see the ground across the street from this height. Canter's head is not angled down—his chair cannot position him in a way that would allow for a view of the street—and we understand that he will never actually see the people whom he has freed reentering society. He had SteepleJack position him in front of the window merely so he could see the passage of time and maybe—just maybe—catch a lucky glimpse of something. Harvey speaks to Canter without looking at him, describing the events on the street.

HARVEY:
HERE THEY COME.

PANEL 4: Harvey's view of the people—real people, not surrogates—that have emerged from the housing units across the street from Canter's building. A few men and women are standing on the sidewalk, not in a group but separate and seemingly oblivious to one another. They wear house clothes, and are of varying age, race, and gender. They are looking around stunned and confused, one of them shading his eyes with his hand because they are not yet adjusted to the sunlight. Again, there is no crowd gathered, just a few individuals, the first to venture timidly into the post-surrogate world.

HARVEY (OP):
THIS IS WHAT YOU WANTED.
YOU'VE CHANGED THE WORLD BACK.

HARVEY (OP):
BUT FOR HOW LONG?

PANEL 5: Back to Harvey and Canter looking out the window as seen in Panel 3.

HARVEY:
MAYBE WELCH IS RIGHT.
MAYBE THE BELL
CAN'T BE UNRUNG,
AND THE WHOLE THING
WILL START ALL OVER AGAIN.

PANEL 6: Same, except Harvey has turned his head to Canter, looking at him as he talks.

HARVEY:
MAYBE NOT.
NOW WE WAIT AND SEE.

HARVEY:
BUT YOU DON'T PLAN
TO BE AROUND
THAT LONG, DO YOU?

PANEL 7: Back to Canter from the front. Harvey's hands are reaching in from panel left and unbuckling the straps that hold the VR link to Canter's head. His head is being jostled a bit as Harvey works on the straps, but his eyes remain fixed on the window.

HARVEY (OP):
THERE REALLY ISN'T ANY POINT
IN TAKING YOU IN.
WASTING AWAY IN THAT CHAIR
IS WORSE THAN ANY SENTENCE
THE PENAL CODE COULD IMPOSE.

PANEL 8: Profile of Canter facing panel left. Harvey is standing behind him, facing us because he has just finished removing the headset. He is hanging it on one of the handles at the top of Canter's chair.

HARVEY:
END IT THE WAY YOU WANT.
YOU'VE DONE YOUR BEST
TO SQUARE THE BOOKS,
SO I SUPPOSE
I OWE YOU THAT MUCH.

STEP 1

In the penciling stage, Brett starts by sketching a rough of each panel in red. He includes the outlines for the panel borders and word balloons that will later be added digitally, just to be sure everything fits. Then he goes over the roughs a second time, firming up the drawings.

STEP 2

Brett scans the pencils into his computer, leaving the red pencil roughs behind in the process. He digitally inks the pencils in Photoshop to tighten up the drawings.

STEP 3

Switching to Painter, Brett fleshes out his inks with values of gray. With scanned-in paint textures working as a middle tone, he models lights and darks to help the drawings appear more three-dimensional and make the world seem more real.

STEP 4

Returning to Photoshop one last time, Brett colors the panels using primarily the burn, dodge, and overlay modes. He also adds digital elements, such as the photograph of the buildings in the background of Panel 4. This blending of photos with hand drawn art is a hallmark of his distinctive style.

STEP 5

In the final stage, Brett cleans up the panel gutters and lays the lettering over the art. As you can see, Panel 8 was eventually redrawn to make the action a little clearer.

THE AD CAMPAIGN

It was always one of our goals to have the future world of *The Surrogates* be as believable as possible. One of the ways we tried to do this was by including supplemental material in each issue—seen at the end of each chapter in this collection—which provides deep background on some of the events and characters in the story. Dave Bissel and Jim Titus (of the aptly named graphic design firm *Bissel & Titus*) were the masterminds behind the convincing look of these pieces, adding such elements as the photocopied appearance of the transcript at the end of Chapter 2 and the hyperlinks that make the e-paper at the end of Chapter 3 seem as if it's being read on a computer screen.

When we were getting the first issue ready for the printer, though, it occurred to us that we'd gone to such great lengths to pack the interior with content that it didn't seem right to throw in the towel on the exterior. What to do with the back cover? In serialized comics, this space is usually reserved for advertisements, so Jim suggested that we create a mock ad campaign for Virtual Self, the fictional company in the story that manufactures surrogates. I'd considered fake ads in the scripting stage, but the farthest I went with the idea was

SHARE YOURSELF
LIFE...ONLY BETTER.
VIRTUAL SELF

to jot down a few trial versions of a corporate slogan. It'd be up to Dave and Jim to create a logo and provide the visuals.

This is where they really shined. First came the logo, a hand silhouetted by the outline of a body, designed in a manner that was futuristic and clean, yet subtly oppressive. Then came the first ad concept, a close-up photograph of a couple wrapped in a lovers' embrace, the Virtual Self slogan etched across the frame. The image was eye-catching and

IMPROVE YOURSELF
LIFE...ONLY BETTER.
VIRTUAL SELF

provocative, everything an ad should be. Best of all, it looked *real.* (Incidentally, that original concept ad bore the slogan "Better Than Real" until we discovered it was already taken—by a manufacturer of adult novelties, no less.

To avoid any unwanted confusion, we made the switch to "Life...Only Better.")

Well, that did it. Something about that first image clicked for me, and I began brainstorming with a series of

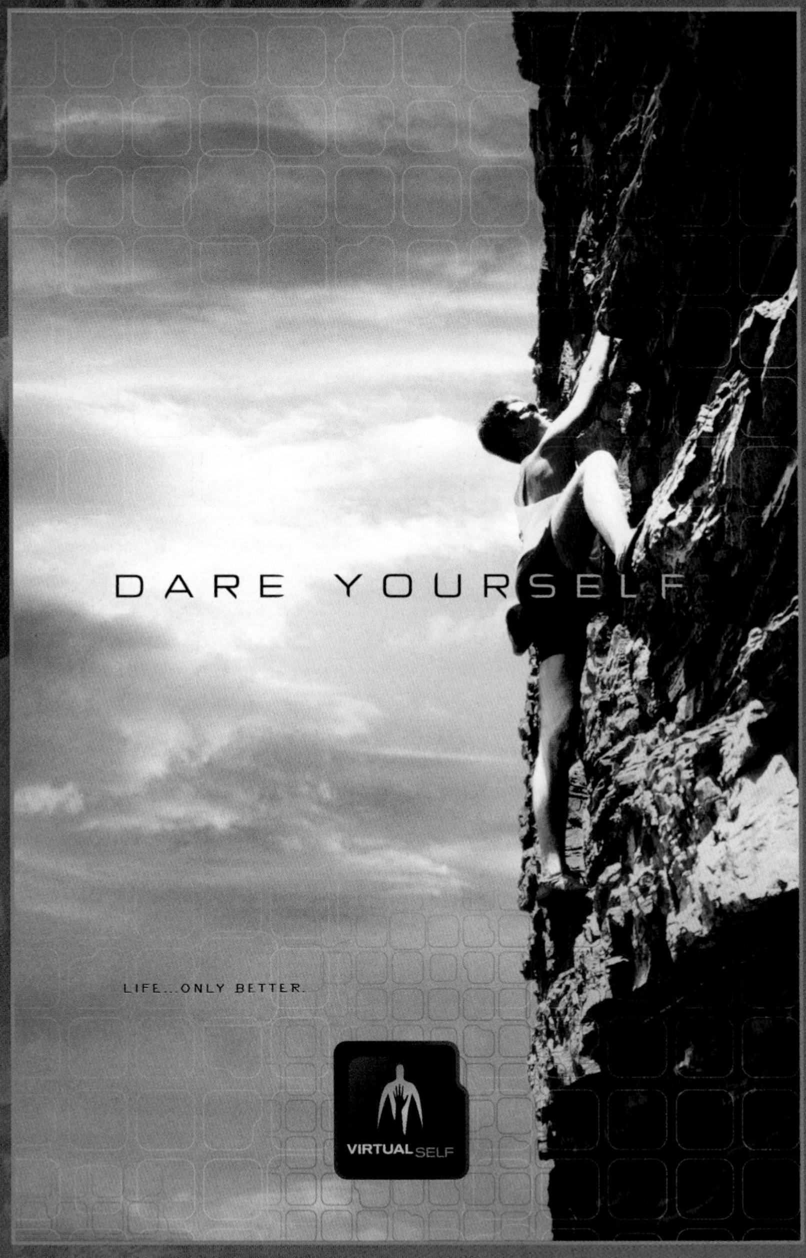

DARE YOURSELF
LIFE...ONLY BETTER.
VIRTUALSELF

different phrases that played on the word "self." Instead of repeating a single slogan throughout the campaign, we could use these phrases as the basis for ads that targeted specific surrogate-buying demographics. "Share Yourself" for the lovers, "Dare Yourself" for extreme sports athletes, "Present Yourself" for business professionals, and so on. We could even tailor each ad to correspond with a character or characters that were encountered in the issue on which it ran.

ENJOY YOURSELF
LIFE...ONLY BETTER.
VIRTUAL SELF

Jim liked this new direction, and he put together a mockup.

After we saw it—the way "self" was accented, the way he'd managed to include both the rotating copy and the repeating slogan—we knew we had something truly unique.

We even carried the theme of the ad campaign over to the brochure supplement in Chapter 4, labeling it "Choose Yourself." The result was better than anything we could have anticipated. The placement of the ads on the back covers,

PRESENT YOURSELF
LIFE...ONLY BETTER.
VIRTUALSELF

combined with their realistic appearance, fooled some readers into thinking Virtual Self was a real company existing in the here and now. It wasn't until we ran the brochure supplement that they realized what we'd done.

DELETED SCENE

Since no behind the scenes tour would be complete without outtakes, here's just one of the many things that got left on the cutting room floor. After SteepleJack's successful theft of the EMP software at the close of Chapter 3, my original story outline had Chapter 4 opening with a newscast, followed by these two pages showing a down-and-out Harvey taking drastic steps to ease his loneliness.

I decided to cut this scene because I felt it was too out of character for Harvey. All along I'd portrayed him as a man of old-fashioned values—and it was well-established that he still carried a serious torch for his wife—so it didn't make sense to show him cruising the strolls. I never forgot about this scene, though, and I jumped at the chance to draft a version of it for inclusion in this collection, where it appears alongside Brett's sketches to give you a glimpse of what almost was.

CHAPTER 4 / PAGE 2 (7 Panels)

PANEL 1: Top tier panel. Night. This is an establishing shot of a street corner in the Backbone District. Harvey's car—not the squad car, but his personal car—is parked at the curb a few feet away from a gathering of four scantily-clad (miniskirts, fishnets, etc.) female prostitutes. The women vary in appearance, but they are all young and alluring in their own way. Three of the women are talking to each other, but the fourth has turned her head to look at the car. The car is parked so that it faces the women, allowing the driver inside to watch them through the front windshield. Positioned near the women is a dim streetlamp that lights the scene.

PANEL 2: Move us to the sidewalk. The three talking women are in the foreground, smiling and gesturing at each other and otherwise ignoring the car. The woman who had her head turned in the above panel has now broken away from the pack, and she is strolling seductively away from us and towards the car. We can see a shadowed figure sitting behind the wheel, but we are too far away to see who it is.

PANEL 3: The woman's POV looking down through the driver's side window of the car. Harvey has rolled the window down and is looking up at her glumly—he's sad that his longing for real human contact has brought him to this.

WOMAN 1 (OP):
HEY THERE, BABY.

HARVEY:
HOW MUCH?

PANEL 4: We're inside the car now. Our POV is such that we are seated in the passenger's seat beside Harvey, looking past him and at the woman. She has bent over at the waist to rest her elbows on the doorframe, and she is smiling at Harvey seductively. Harvey's head is turned towards the woman. He is alarmed by her forwardness—he's not used to these types of situations—and he recoils a little.

WOMAN 1:
WELL, THAT DEPENDS ON WHAT
YOU'RE ASKING FOR, DOESN'T IT?

PANEL 5: Same shot, but Harvey is no longer recoiling. The woman cocks her head to the side playfully.

WOMAN 1:
I GOT A NICE ROOM AT THE SHERWOOD ARMS WHERE
WE CAN TALK ALL ABOUT IT. IT'S JUST AROUND THE CORNER.

WOMAN 1:
WHAT DO YOU SAY?

PANEL 6: Move back outside the car now. We're standing to the left of the woman, looking past her and at Harvey. He looks back at her with a pained expression.

HARVEY:
HOW ABOUT YOUR PLACE INSTEAD?

WOMAN 1:
HONEY, AS FAR AS YOU'RE CONCERNED,
THE SHERWOOD IS MY PLACE.
I DON'T MAKE A HABIT OF LETTING TRICKS
KNOW WHERE I LIVE.

PANEL 7: Rotate the camera again, and zoom in for a close shot of Harvey and the woman in profile, facing each other through the open window. Harvey looks at her sheepishly.

HARVEY:
YOU SURE? I'M WILLING TO PAY EXTRA.

WOMAN 1:
YOU'D HAVE TO BE, BUT IT'S LIKE I SAID—

WOMAN 1:
WAIT A MINUTE . . .

PAGE 3 (7 Panels)

PANEL 1: Close shot from the front of the woman's head and shoulders. Her eyes narrow skeptically—the playfulness is gone.

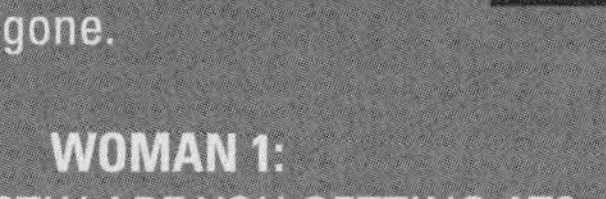

WOMAN 1:
WHAT EXACTLY ARE YOU GETTING AT?

PANEL 2: Switch to a close-up of Harvey's face. His expression hasn't changed, but something about the sadness in it drives the point home—he wants the real deal.

PANEL 3: Back to the woman. We see her from the front again, but this is a wider shot, so that we see her from the waist up. She is standing upright and pulling her arms towards herself, as if she is backing away from something dangerous—now it is her turn to recoil. This is Harvey's POV, so we should see her at a slight upward angle.

WOMAN 1:
UH UH. NO WAY.
WHAT ARE YOU, SOME KIND OF FREAK?

PANEL 4: We are standing at the front bumper of the car now. We see Harvey through the windshield, and the woman is standing at panel right. She has turned at the waist to yell back at the women who are off-panel behind us. Harvey looks up at her with a panicked expression, waving his hands about—he doesn't want her to announce his intentions.

WOMAN 1:
HEY, ROSIE! GET A LOAD
OF WHAT THIS SICKO JUST TOLD ME.

HARVEY:
PLEASE DON'T—

WOMAN 1:
HE SAID HE'LL PAY EXTRA FOR A SKINJOB.

PANEL 5: Switch to the other women. One of them—Rosie—is walking towards us, a sarcastic look on her face. In the background we see the remaining two women have stopped talking and turned their heads to look off-panel at Harvey contemptuously.

ROSIE:
NOW THERE'S ONE I HAVEN'T HEARD IN A WHILE.
THIS I HAVE TO SEE FOR MYSELF.

PANEL 6: Back to the angle in Panel 4. Harvey has turned away from the window, and he is frantically trying to drop the car into gear. Rosie is next to the car now, and she has bent over to get a better look at Harvey through the driver's side window. The other woman stands to Rosie's right. Her arms are crossed and she looks down at Harvey angrily.

ROSIE:
HEY, HAVEN'T I SEEN YOU SOMEWHERE?

ROSIE:
SURE, I NEVER FORGET A FACE. YOU WERE AT THE PRECINCT LAST TIME I GOT ARRESTED. YOU'RE A COP. YOU USED TO BE THINNER, THOUGH . . .

PANEL 7: Rotate the camera, so that we're behind the car as it drives away from us. The two women stand on the curb at panel left, watching the car speed off. Rosie's hands are on her hips, and the posture of both women tells us that they are offended, of all things.

WOMAN 1:
A COP? AS IF THEY DON'T HAVE
BETTER THINGS TO DO THAN COME
AROUND HERE HARASSING US.

ROSIE:
YOU SHOULD'VE KNOWN. NOBODY IN THEIR
RIGHT MIND WOULD ASK FOR THAT.

PINUP GALLERY

Becky Cloonan

Farel Dalrymple

Kieron Dwyer

Duncan Fegredo

MATT KINDT

LIVEWIRE

THE FUTURE OF SCIENCE-FICTION

IN THIS ISSUE:
STEEPLEJACK THE MANIAC SURRIE-KILLER STRIKES AGAIN!

A full-length novella.

KINDT2005!

Steve Lieber

MAH
FOOD
2005

Greg Ruth

Michael Sincavage

Jim Titus

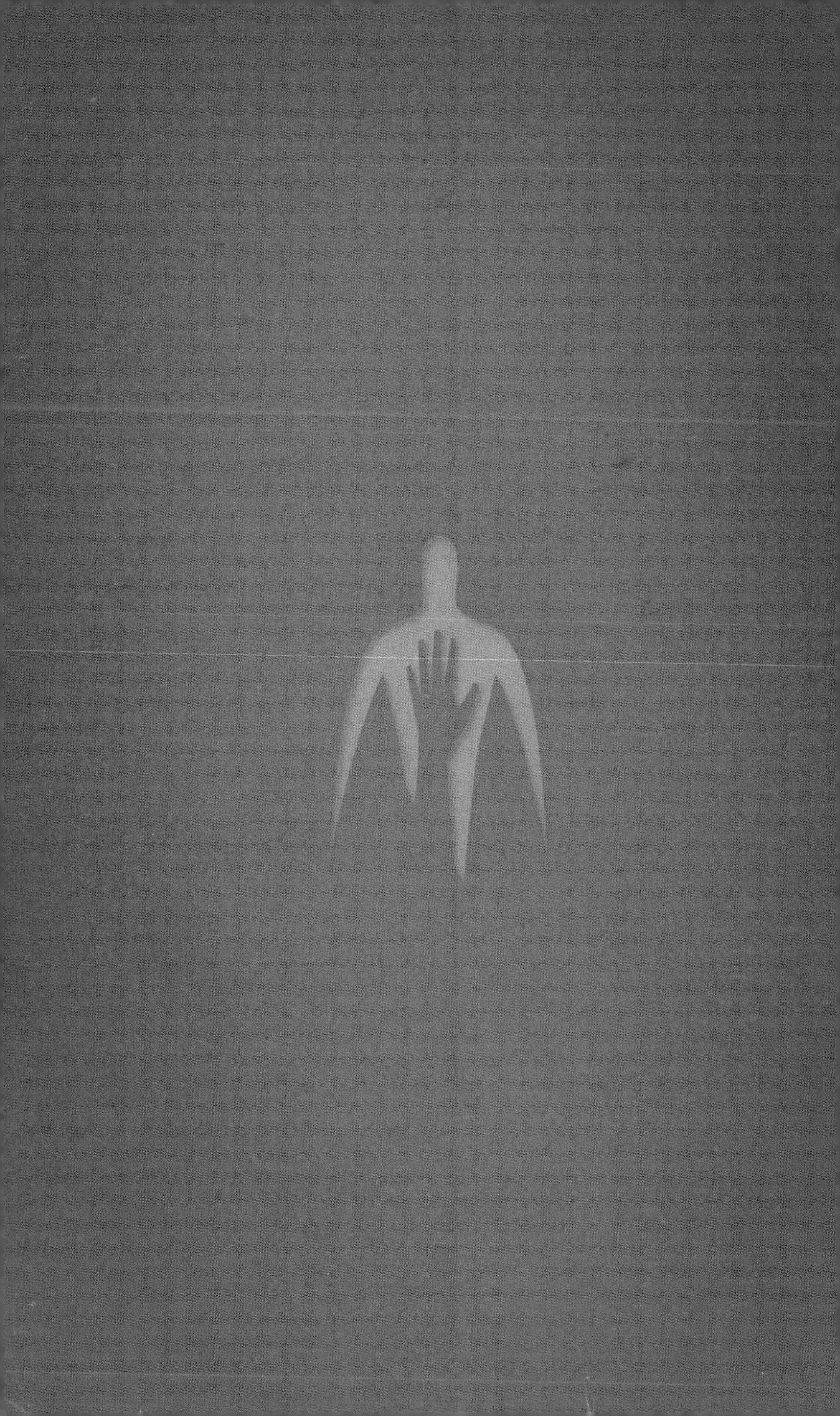